Billy Lane's Encyclopaedia of Float Fishing

Billy Lane's Encyclopaedia of Float Fishing

Billy Lane & Colin Graham

PELHAM BOOKS

First published in Great Britain by
PELHAM BOOKS LTD
52 Bedford Square
*London, W.C.*1
JUNE 1971
SECOND IMPRESSION FEBRUARY 1972

7207 0514 2

Printed by Hollen Street Press Ltd at Slough
and bound by Dorstel Press at Harlow, Essex

To John Ingham
with thanks for all his encouragement

Contents

Illustrations

Preface

All the ideas in this book are Billy's. They stem from a knowledge of float fishing techniques which, in my experience, few could equal. Some years ago, it was decided that knowledge of this calibre ought not to go to waste, the happy result being that I was given the privilege of talking and fishing with Billy so that I could put his knowledge into words for him. It proved to be an experience which was both educational and pleasurable ... for Billy, I soon discovered, was just about the friendliest angler you could ever hope to meet and, more important, one who was prepared to share all his knowledge with no little secrets held back.

At that time, many of the floats we tell you about here were new to me. So, to help me grasp the principles behind them correctly, we decided that it was vital that I learn how to fish with every single one of them. The result, for me, was an improvement in my own angling abilities and, with the publication of this book, we would like to think that coarse fishermen everywhere will find something in it which will help them improve their techniques, too.

We would both like to thank Ken Whiteley and Michael Williams for the patient way in which they prepared the diagrams for us and to *Angler's Mail*, and John Ingham in particular, for permission to publish them here.

COLIN GRAHAM

Introduction

For most coarse fishermen their idea of angling happiness is to sit quietly watching a float. For so many, it seems the ideal way of fishing and the one which brings them most pleasure.

Latterly, however, there has been a swing to the leger, usually allied with several methods of bite indication of which the swing tip is perhaps now the most famous.

Such has been the impact of this trend it has tended to cast doubts—wrongly in my opinion—on the efficiency of the float in many waters and conditions. All of which is a shame because such a picture is a false one.

Floats are still as good as ever they were in coping with most conditions and waters an angler may encounter. The current craze for the tip amounts to the fact that in certain waters the fish have become preoccupied with baits presented in this way.

Nevertheless, there are still large numbers of anglers—and I am one of them—who still have faith in the float and it is to all of them that this book is respectfully dedicated.

In it I present all the floats I use, floats which, I maintain, allow me to cope with every eventuality.

It has been a difficult job for in recent times new floats, sometimes involving tricky techniques, have joined the ever-growing arsenal of equipment we use these days in the hunt for bigger and better catches.

Zoomers, Sliders, Sticks, Duckers and Avons ... these are but a few of the names we have to conjure with nowadays. To some this ever-increasing variety has been something they have been able to take in their stride. But, for many more, the rapid improvement in float techniques has led to frustration and this is something I hope will be cured for you by reading this book.

In its pages you will find floats old and new. The important thing about them is that as far as I am concerned they are sufficient for any angler to fish every kind of water in the country for every sort of fish—big or small.

Every one of them has stood me in good stead in practical angling conditions over years of successful fishing and any float included here has passed this test and is still doing an important job for me.

But before taking you, logically I hope, through the various patterns I use I'd like to set down a few basic thoughts about floats which I think will help the reader understand more easily what follows.

And I would first like to knock a failing I have found in many anglers. They have a pet float. Regardless of where they are or what they are fishing for that's the float that goes on.

What usually happens is that on one particular day they have caught a lot of fish with this float and, by some weird deduction of their own, have gone on to invest it with some kind of magic power seeing it almost as an automatic passport to success. Goodness only knows how many wasted fishing hours this has cost them!

If you have got a pet float complex get it in perspective now. If it's a float that fulfils a particular purpose, still use it for that job and that job alone.

If, like so many floats, it just looks good and is of the type so commonly seen these days which is meant to catch anglers rather than fish, then chuck it away.

For me a float has three specific jobs to do: (1) simply to register the bite; (2) to help present the bait; (3) to help you keep in full control of your tackle. And those points are given in order of importance.

Looking at them in detail, the float is the only means of getting in contact with the fish when float fishing and, therefore, it must register the bite as perfectly as possible.

To make sure bites come it follows that the bait must be presented as naturally as conditions permit. The right float —correctly shotted—is essential.

Having assured accurate bite detection and proper bait

presentation the angler must still be in full control of his tackle and the problem here is usually the weather. Once again it is the float which can solve this problem for you.

All this may seem elementary to more experienced readers but, in fact, it is remarkable how many anglers overlook these basic facts. So remember, the float must be the right one from three points of view and if it doesn't satisfy all these functions a change must be made.

Just as important is the choice of material used for making the float. Two key factors play a part here—sensitivity and buoyancy.

It's all too easy to have a float that is sensitive but, at the same time, too buoyant. To give a simple example, a sensitive float in turbulent water will give too many false bites.

So, in considering materials for making floats, I find it best to look at them from two points of view, the material for making the stem and the material for making the body of the float.

For me the most used material for stems these days are cane, wire and certain of the quills. Of these, I now use cane more than any other.

For bodies four materials are most often used, balsa, cork, pith and plastic.

I reject plastic myself because while it can be very sensitive it doesn't seem to have any buoyancy. Though not absolutely against pith, I still have reservations about it on the grounds that it is too buoyant.

So that leaves balsa and cork and these, you will discover, are the two materials I most favour for float bodies these days.

There will be anglers who would quarrel with these findings but, as I have tried to emphasise already, this question of choice is an extremely personal thing.

The most important thing is that whatever float you use you really understand why it is doing the job you want it to do. You must know what movements of that float constitute a bite—and I am thinking of movements other than the simple submerging of the tip—and why that movement means what it does.

I cannot emphasise this strongly enough. The pet floats I mentioned earlier are often the only ones the anglers who use them understand in their selection. This is why in terms of float fishing technique so many of them are standing still.

In the following chapters I have treated the floats in a logical sequence starting with the simplest float for the simplest conditions and going on from there to the more complex ones.

In following them through I am sure you will notice the very real developments there have been and I think it worth mentioning that many of them would simply not have been possible had it not been for the introduction of monofilament line. This truly opened new horizons for the experimental float angler.

Being something of a veteran myself now, my experience runs right through from the old silk lines to monofilament and because I fished through this vital time of change, it does, I feel, give me a proper perspective of the way float fishing has developed.

Some of the floats I shall tell you about will be what one might term 'specialist' types and you may find that well-made versions of these patterns are not all that easy to come by in tackle shops. Don't accept second best or it will only bring you more frustration. Keep looking for good examples or better still, make them yourself. The diagrams and photographs should tell you most of what you need to know.

Chapter *1*

The crowquill

The development of floats for coarse fishing over the years has probably been one of the most logical in our sport ... starting off from simple beginnings, then becoming ever more complex as time went on, with the greatest leaps forward being made after the introduction of monofilament lines.

Being, I hope, a fairly logical sort of chap, I decided that the best way to help you understand the many methods which can be used with floats would be to follow that same logical line of development.

So we'll start with the grand-daddy of all the floats—the crowquill.

No float is more simple than this one. None more delicate. In ideal conditions on the right sort of water, it's unbeatable, a fact which explains why the crowquill has probably been used by anglers longer than any other kind of float.

And yet the strange thing is that many modern anglers have discarded the crowquill. I know many who have never used it at all, having dismissed it as somehow 'old hat'.

Being in the trade myself, I have the chance to watch at first hand the way in which many anglers go for the new and pretty float in preference to something much less glamorous, which almost invariably would do a better job. There are more anglers caught by a pretty float than there are fish, I can tell you!

But let's start on the evidence which, I submit, makes the crowquill a must in any self-respecting angler's tackle box.

As you will discover there's more than one form of crow-

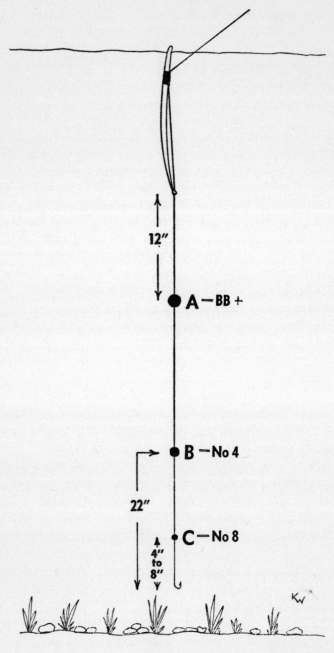

Fig. 1

quill float and more than one way of fishing them.

I intend to begin with the simplest form of all used for the simplest purpose, stillwater fishing (see Fig. 1). The advantages of the float should be obvious. It's slim; so slim that it offers little or no resistance to the water or to the fish, despite the fact that it has an extremely buoyant tip.

The rig shown is the way you would set up the quill for fairly close-in fishing in stillwater in ideal conditions. The day you'd use this set-up there would be no surface drag, no strong wind, in fact nothing extreme about the conditions at all. In other words, a dreamy day.

Look first at the way the float—anything between 5 in. and 8 in. long—is fixed to the line. This is the first important thing to get right. The line passes through a valve rubber about an inch from the tip and then down through the eyelet ring. This is the most natural way to fish it, with the thickest part at the top.

The water we are fishing won't be more than 6 ft. deep. Above that depth the simple crowquill would be rejected and a different float needed—a float I shall be describing later.

The biggest shot (A in the diagram) is only 12 in. below the float. It's put there to aid casting—to make sure the terminal tackle enters the water BEFORE the float—and also to make certain the float cocks as soon as possible to give you the earliest possible indication of a bite.

Shot B in the diagram is always in the same position and this, too, helps casting. Shot B and shot C, which completes the weighting, also help the natural fall of the bait through the water.

With the shots set like this you get a smooth cast, a trouble-free entry and a natural fall to the bait. Three things happen after entry. Shot A registers on the float first and it sinks a bit. Then shot B weighs in, sinking it a little more. Finally shot C brings the float down until little more than an eighth of an inch of the tip is showing.

It's most important to get used to watching out for these three different registers. Most bites are likely to come after the third register, but you can get them sooner. When this happens the register of shot A or B will be delayed. Strike the moment you notice this! In other words, if the sequence you have come to know is not going according to plan, the assumption, every time, must be that the cause is a fish ... a factor worth remembering with most floats.

The emphasis is on shot C as the most decisive one of all. What happens to this shot mostly decides how the bite will be indicated to you. Generally, the fish will swim away with the bait after the tackle has gone through the three settings. In that case the bite will be signalled by the submerging of the float.

If, on the other hand, the fish takes the bait in a way which takes the weight of shot C off the float—by moving up in the water with it—the float will lift to signal the bite. This is particularly true in stillwater, when the fish come up to meet the bait much more often than they would in running water. Look out for those lifts—you're likely to cop for a lot of them!

I hope much of this will have helped to explain the variable measurement of 4 in. to 18 in. of shot C to the hook. This, too, is a vital factor in efficient bite detection.

Let's say small roach are playing with the bait when you have shot C set at 18 in. The result will be little tips and taps on the float with nothing positive developing. That's the signal to move the shot nearer the hook. It's a question of trial and error. A good yardstick is to always start with shot C 18 in. from the hook and then take action when you've watched developments. Eventually shot C will reach a position when, although you will still get a prelude of tip-taps, there will eventually follow a positive indication.

What I have said so far applies to fishing the bait just off the bottom—as in the diagram. The same rig can be varied slightly to fish on the bottom—laying-on as it's called. Before explaining this I'd like to stress that you'd need even more perfect conditions to do this properly. It follows that if you allow shot C to rest on the bottom you could snag or bury the bait when you want your bait on the bottom, not IN it.

The best way to achieve this is to start with shot C 12 in. from the hook. Set the float higher up the line and try a sample cast. If more than an eighth of an inch is showing after the tackle has settled you know shot C must be on the bottom. Move the float back down the line and try again until you have found the critical point at which the tip gives the right amount of 'show' … in other words shot C is probably an inch off the bottom while the bait is lying on it.

Before summing up, a word about the size of the float. I mentioned 5 in. to 8 in. The criteria for deciding which to use is simple—the nearer the bank you are fishing the smaller the float. Don't forget that as you reduce the size of the float the shot, too, must be reduced, although still fixed to the line in the same scale and pattern.

Where would you use this simplest of all crowquill rigs —and where should you forget about it?

Never use it on water more than 6 ft. deep. Never use it in fast running water. Never use it in rough weather. Never use it where long casting is needed.

The right kind of places? Any pond or lake where those conditions are absent. Any normal canal like the Staffordshire, the Lancaster or the Oxford—the small narrow jobs. But there's a rider here. Remember there should be little or no flow. A different setting, as you will see later, is needed when this is the case.

The crowquill in the form I'm talking about is for sensitive fishing in kind conditions. If you treat it right it will do all you ask of it. Expect too much of it and you'll only meet frustration.

Before I tell you how the simple crowquill can be used for certain running waters, I'd like to tell you why the crowquill has come to gain such an affectionate place in my float wallet and why, over the years, I've come to reject all the other forms of quill float—used on their own, that is.

The only time I ever use a porcupine quill—as you will discover later in this book—is as a sliding float. I'd never use it in the simple form you see in so many tackle shops.

Peacock quills, goosequills, you can have, too—and any others you can think of. I am not against these materials by blind prejudice. I don't want to know about them for a reason which, to me, has become apparent over years of experience. The great disadvantage of the porcupine—and quills like it—is that its weight in proportion to the shot on the terminal tackle is invariably heavier than with the crowquill. The net result of this discrepancy is that there is a great tendency for the float to overcast with the end tackle finishing up in a tangle behind the float. With the crowquill, the shot invariably precede the float into the water—which is the way it should be.

My objection to porcupine quills rests solely on the way they can interfere with smooth casting. And for me that's reason enough to stay faithful to the crowquill.

Cane has been used as an alternative to crowquill but here again I'm not too keen. This material on its own doesn't give a nice, even sinking action after the float has hit the water. Cane floats often lie flat after the cast and you have to jiggle the line to persuade them to cock ... a time-wasting procedure which could cost you a missed bite, something I'm always happy to do without!

By now, I hope you have been persuaded about the very real merits of the crowquill and are ready to hear how this basic float can be used in running water as opposed to still. First I think I had better make it quite clear what I mean by running water in this context. It's no good trying to use the simple crowquill in heavy or turbulent water. It just won't wear it.

Basically, you need water that is not running too fast and, even more important, is flowing smoothly. There should be no boils or turbulence of any kind in the swim. Weatherwise, the wind should not be strong.

Having found the right swim and the right conditions you should go on to discover that this is where the crowquill can be used to its greatest advantage. Its perfect slim body enables you to strike at the fish offering less resistance to it than any other float. There's not the slightest danger of the float getting in the way of you and the fish!

The float is fixed to the line the same way—through a valve rubber at the top and down to the terminal tackle via the bottom ring.

It's in the shotting where changes are made. Because of the movement in the water, the shot are put farther down to make the bait sink faster. If you used the same shotting pattern I gave you earlier it's quite likely the bait would pass through your swim without ever reaching the lower depths, where almost invariably you would expect the fish to lie.

To achieve this speedier fall the heaviest shot (A in Fig. 2) is pinched on just 24 in. above the hook—a position which helps it to do its job of getting the bait down without offering any resistance to a taking fish. The dust shot which previously was last on our line has now been eliminated and its place (point B) has been taken by a three-times-heavier No. 4 shot.

This is still part of the plan to get the bait down quickly while offering no worries in terms of resistance. The extra weight of this shot is offset by the pull of the water and its real impact on the fish is no more than the dust shot would be in stillwater.

Again a variable measurement—from four to 18 in.—is given for this shot and, as in stillwater, the reason is the same: to overcome shy bites. The less distinct they are the nearer shot B should be moved to the hook. Eventually, you'll find the right spot after repeated swims where even shy-biting fish will take the float firmly down below the surface.

This has an added advantage in running water. Not only does it show firm downward pulls better, it also makes 'lift' bites materialise more.

Bites of this variety are likely to be most common with this setting of the crowquill when small hook fishing with maggots for roach. Because of the loose feed you are invariably offering, the fish are hovering above the bottom literally waiting for the maggots. When they take the one on the hook they momentarily pause for a moment with their fins work-

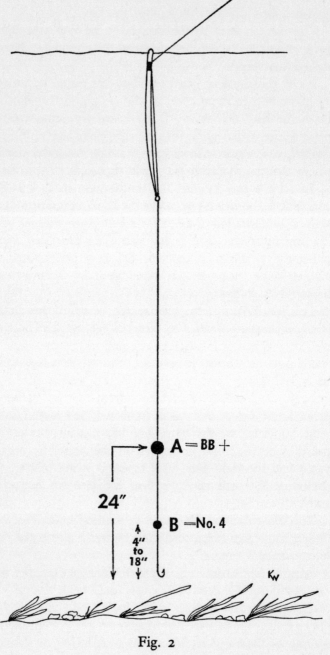

Fig. 2

ing like a brake. It's this that gives you the lift bite.

This rig can be varied for laying-on in running water—an alternative I'm inclined to employ a lot more than I would in stillwater. The big difference is that the bottom shot (B) will always be fished on the bottom. For this method it should never be less than 18 in. from the hook.

In addition, you will need to fish over the real depth of the water. How much is something I have a little formula for and this seems to have served me well over the years. Briefly, I fish a foot over the depth for every 4 ft. of water. If the swim was 8 ft. deep I'd set the float 10 ft. from the hook.

With the tackle set like this you'll see that a fair amount of terminal line is actually lying along the bed of the river, including, not too far from the point where the line goes up to shot A, the lower shot B. Should you find that the tackle is not laying-on firmly enough an additional BB shot can be pinched on alongside A. Despite the fact that this should prove too much for the float to carry you will find you are laid on even more firmly with both shot supported. The only proviso—to keep the float steady and prevent it sinking under—is to keep your rod tip in the air with the line running tight to the float, the method many call 'stret-pegging'.

While the rod can be held in the hand to achieve this, I think it's better to support it in a rest, particularly as bites with this rig are so positive it is easy to get hold of the rod in time to hit them cleanly. Without exception a bite will take the float clean under. There are no wobbles or lifts with this method.

For this to succeed it's best if the tackle is thrown downstream and slightly out from the bank and then drawn back to the rod rest. This has the advantage of straightening out the tackle from the rod tip to hook. You might find, especially with the extra BB on, that the float hasn't surfaced. In this case all you need to do is give a little more line from the reel and up the float will come.

I would never, by the way, choose to lay-on in running water from the outset. I always start by swimming the stream and it is only when I feel certain bites are not going to come with this method that I revert to laying-on.

In terms of size I never use the smaller crowquills for running water. Usually my float will be between 7 in. and 8 in. long—for swimming the stream or laying-on.

The crowquill is the float for ideal conditions ... and, as it is these conditions which most often bring the best catches, that's probably the main reason why it holds such a happy position in the catalogue of floats.

Having said that, don't think we are finished with the crowquill ... far from it. So far I've only told you about its simplest uses.

Chapter 2

The reverse crowquill—darts—onions

Having spent a chapter indoctrinating you into the idea of the crowquill, I am now going to turn those thoughts upside down. But don't worry. It's all in the good cause of catching fish. I am talking now about the reverse crowquill, a variant of the simple float I've just discussed which helps us achieve more with this material.

As its name suggests, this float is made so that the quill fishes upside down with the ring at the thick end and the tip at the thin one.

It has two main advantages over the simple crowquill. It will carry a little more lead and therefore extend the limit of your casting distance. And with such a fine tip the resistance of the float to a surface wind is considerably reduced.

From this it should be obvious you can fish with it in rougher conditions than you can with the simple crowquill. The one disadvantage is that it can only be used in still water. That's because it is literally so sensitive that it's constantly going under in running water, giving you more false bites than true ones.

Let's give an example of when to use it. You are on a lake using a simple crowquill when a wind springs up. Suddenly you find your casting distance reduced. There's too much ripple. Worse still, the surface drag is going one way, the undertow the opposite way.

All these things can be overcome by the reverse float, in

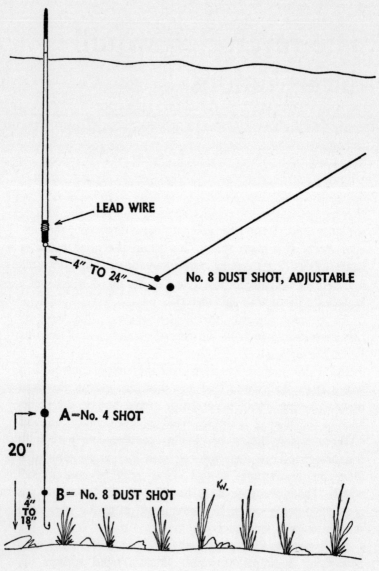

LEAD WIRE

4" TO 24"

No. 8 DUST SHOT, ADJUSTABLE

A=No. 4 SHOT

20"

4"
TO
18"

B= No. 8 DUST SHOT

KW.

Fig. 3

a way which should allow you to continue casting to the same baited areas.

For, unlike the simple version, the reverse quill buries your line under the surface. A quick glance at the diagram (Fig. 3) should make this clear. Just exactly how it works is something I'll be telling you in a moment. It's enough to say at this stage that this sinking of the line is often one of the most important factors of all in float-fishing and one you'll find me referring to again and again.

Once more, there's a limit to the depth of water in which to use this float. I'd put it at no more than 5 ft. Above that I think you'll find the float too light to carry the amount of lead you'd need.

The float depicted in the diagram is about 7 in. long and is the only size of reverse crowquill I use. Correctly weighted it shows one inch at the tip—and the set-up is so finely balanced that the addition of one tiny dust shot would be sufficient to submerge it completely.

The efficiency of this float varies according to the bait. It's at its best with maggots or with bread and other cereals but not nearly so effective with worm, when the weight of the bait can upset the finely calculated shotting.

All floats used to bury the line and beat the wind are fished from the bottom. In this instance part of the plan involves lead wire which you can see wrapped round the float just above the end ring. The lead wire should be fine —but no so fine it will become unwound with use.

Getting this exactly right is essential—and best done before you go fishing. Here's how to do it. Pass a loop of nylon through the float ring and pinch on the total number of shot shown in the diagram—one No. 4 and two dust. Put the float in a bath or tub of water with the loop suspended and then add lead wire until the tip of the float is showing $1\frac{1}{4}$ in. I know I said earlier that the float, when fishing, would show one inch. It will. That extra $\frac{1}{4}$ in. in the bath is to allow for the weight of your line.

When you've completed this test keep the loop of shot with the float in your wallet—then you'll know beyond doubt that everything is going to be exactly balanced when you go to fish.

Having got that right, the next thing to talk about is attaching the float to the line ... a thing many anglers make a mess of. So often they end up with a knot which doesn't allow free movement of the float up and down the line—so vital for coping with changes in depth.

To get it right, pass the line through the eyelet ring and hold it back against the float. Then pass it through again. Hold both strands back. Do this four times. The important thing is never to pass the line between the ring and one of the previous turns. Holding the turns back firmly prevents this. Despite the fact that you've made four turns the float should move easily and freely.

Another odd thing is the number of anglers I've seen using this float fixed top and bottom. They must be crazy for they are defeating all the objects it was intended to achieve.

First, their line isn't buried. Second, the resistance of a reverse quill on the strike is increased enormously. In fact, you are hitting the float first and NOT the fish. With the bottom ring attachment the float collapses smoothly out of the way on the strike and you are straight into the fish.

The shotting—with one exception—is similar to that for orthodox crowquill fishing (Fig. 3 again). Any bulk shotting up the line has been eliminated by the use of lead wire which has made the float semi self-cocking. Shot 'A' is positioned there to complete the vertical setting and to carry the bait down to the fish reasonably quickly. Dust shot 'B' is our tell-tale for bites and should be set within the limits given according to the strength of the bites. The shyer they are the nearer it is moved to the hook.

The exception is the second dust shot between the float and the rod tip. Its sole purpose is to enable the line to be buried quickly, defeating the wind's pull on the surface and the drag underneath. To gain the greatest efficiency from this shot the rod tip should be kept just under or very near the surface after casting.

Where you place this shot depends on the distance you are fishing from the bank and the speed at which you want to sink the line. The farther the cast the farther this shot should be from the float.

At its nearest setting, four inches from the float, you would be fishing not more than one rod length out. This shot has another advantage, particularly when set at the maximum 24 in. from the float ring. It enables you to move the bait slowly and naturally through the water with the minimum disturbance of the tackle. All you have to do is to give a twitch on the line with your reel.

The setting in the diagram is for fishing off the bottom. To lay-on with the reverse crowquill it's necessary to make alterations in the shotting. Shot 'B' for this technique should certainly be no less than 18 in. from the hook and there's nothing to stop you making it much more. The main thing to remember is that shot 'A' and the float must be moved up the line the same distance.

You can tell you have got it right because the float will sit a little higher in the water after the cast, returning to its normal 'show' of 1 in. when shot 'B' has reached the bottom. But, as I've said before, I have reservations about fishing in still water with the lower shot on the bottom because of weeds and things. So, mostly, I fish with it just off the bed—in which case the 'show' on the float will be normal.

Used properly the reverse crowquill is a handy gadget to have. But like all crowquills, it must be treated with respect and too much must never be asked of it.

For ponds and lakes in reasonable conditions it's just the job. In canals more care must be taken. The water should be still or moving only at the most sluggish rate. With any appreciable flow at all, forget it.

Now while the reverse crowquill still has many loyal fans and is still an efficient performer of the task it was designed for, I have recently found myself also favouring a new float which has only recently come into general use. The float—aptly named—is called the Dart and it is a most useful

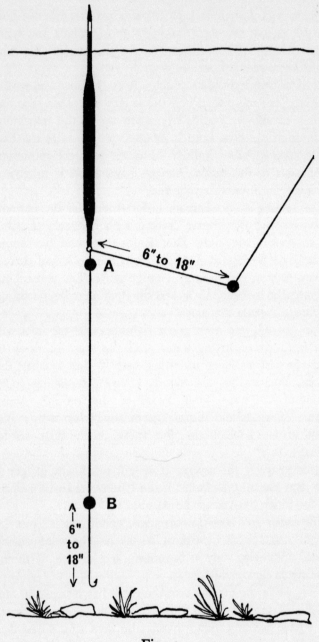

6" to 18"

A

B

6"
to
18"

Fig. 4

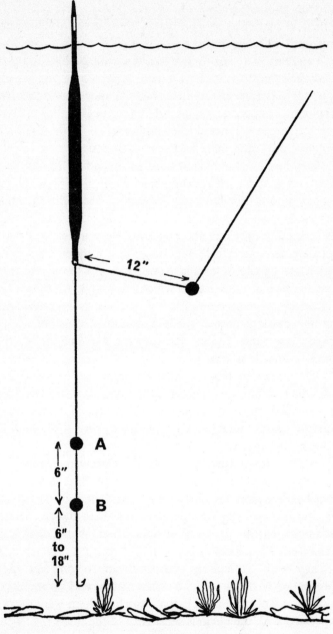

12"

A

6"

B

6"
to
18"

Fig. 5

C

addition to the floats we use for still waters and, especially, canals, in particular as an efficient alternative to the reverse crowquill with the added merit that it is easier to use.

The Dart, as I see it, is even more acceptable, however, because it does everything the reverse crowquill will do and more. It's more sensitive. It's easier to shot up (the reverse crowquill, remember, required fiddling about with lead wire). Because it's straight, it eliminates the 'lean' there was with the crowquill and, finally, it casts easier.

Look now at our diagrams (Figs. 4 and 5) of the Dart which is a semi self-cocking float made that way by the introduction of just the right amount of loading in the stem needed to make it sit in the water correctly. The stem (which also gives the float that short antenna you can see) is 1/16th in. diameter cane which is fitted into a slender balsa body which has parallel sides and is loaded at the lower end with a short piece of brass rod to which the ring is whipped.

Like the reverse crowquill, the Dart is fished loose with the line passing through the end ring only, thus giving one exactly the same facility for burying the line under the surface when it is windy.

Darts come in three different lengths each having five different loadings, i.e. they carry exactly one, two, three, four or five dust shots, a statement which should immediately impress on you that the Dart works to very fine limits in terms of sensitivity.

To give credit where it is due, the Dart was inspired, to the best of my knowledge, by a type of float devised by Lancashire anglers for bloodworm fishing and, in particular, by that group who are perhaps the best-known British exponents of this style, those lads from Wigan who call themselves 'The Firm'.

They were particularly successful not so long ago in a number of matches on the Leamington and Warrington canals and Coventry anglers who watched them were deeply impressed with the obvious sensitivity of the floats they were using. At the same time they reckoned that, if developed, the floats they saw could have wider applications than being used solely for bloodworms. While still retaining the original line and, with it, the float's sensitivity, there was no reason why the float should not be scaled up to enable its use for maggots, caster and that other favourite canal bait, punched bread, and then fished over fair distances.

The original idea then was The Firm's and they deserve all the credit for the basic pattern. Others have now developed it further into the shape in which I am now suggesting you should try it.

The Dart, as its name suggests, is fine on the cast going straight through the air like an arrow, due, mainly, to the loading in the stem.

So far so good. But the next most important, and obvious, question is when to use which size, especially as the choice seems so wide. Several factors play a part.

The first—and, you might think, the most obvious—is distance. But funnily enough such is the streamlined design of these floats all three sizes are just as capable of the maximum amount of travel any canal angler could want. And almost the same goes for still waters.

The real reason then for three sizes is, in fact, the degree of line sinking one wants to achieve between rod tip and float. The more you want to bury that line because of wind the longer the Dart you select.

In this respect depth also plays a part. The longest of the three floats is seven inches and obviously you wouldn't want to use one this long in a canal which was only two or three feet deep. In such a situation you would obviously opt for the smaller length.

Now, as I mentioned earlier, each of these three sizes offers five loadings in terms of dust shots making for a total range of 15 floats. I think—though others disagree with me—that this is too many for I find it difficult to imagine any circumstances except one of utter desperation when I would feel inclined to use a one dust shot version.

In such an instance, the water would be gin clear and I would be after fishing an extremely slow falling bait in conditions which would have to be absolutely perfect, demonstration enough, I feel, of the limitations of the lightest loading with this float.

Personally, I prefer to work only with those Darts which carry from three dust shots up, and the reason is this. I want a bit of leeway when it comes to burying that line, the sort which will permit me to put a back shot my side of the float to help that line burying process. The float that carries only one or even two dust shots cramps my style extremely if I want to do this. But with three—or more—dust shots to permutate, it can be easily done.

Darts, despite their light loading, permit you to cast with greater freedom. You can put more thump into it compared with other canal floats and particularly, it must be admitted, when compared with the reverse crowquill. The latter was best cast underhand or tangles were often the result. The Dart can be cast as you like—underhand, over, sideways—in complete safety.

There remains the question of placement of the shot. In normal conditions, with little wind or flow, our first diagram (Fig. 4) is the one which gives you our pattern. Shot B, your tell-tale, moves nearest the hook when bites are shyest. Shot A, to give stability, goes directly under the float. The back shot is fixed farther from the float the stronger the drag.

If it's breezy our second diagram (Fig. 5) gives you the changes. Shot A drops to a position 6 in. above the tell-tale to help guard against back tangles while the back shot is always at 12 in. from the float. The tell-tale B, finds its place as before. Now obviously both these diagrams cover only the three dust shot pattern. What happens when four or five are used? The answer is simply that all the extra shot are added at position A in both cases.

For laying-on, adjust the tackle so that there is an 18 in. terminal tail below shot B, the shot itself being just *off* the bottom.

That, then, is the Dart. In my opinion, an improvement on the reverse crowquill but one which does not mean the reverse float is no longer of use.

From an alternative to a crowquill, the Dart, back now to another form of the quill itself.

'Know your onions' is a favourite expression among

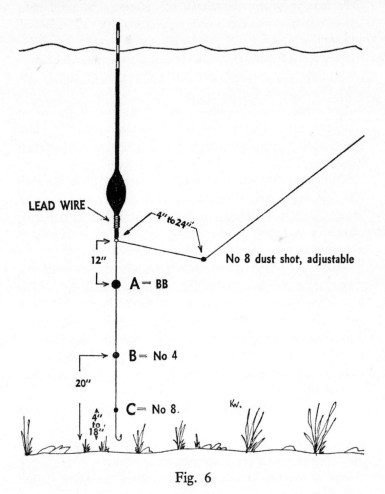

LEAD WIRE

4" to 24"

No 8 dust shot, adjustable

12"

A = BB

B = No 4

20"

C = No 8.

4" to 18"

Kw.

Fig. 6

anglers in the Midlands and when they say it they are not talking about something to eat!

They are referring to yet another version of the crowquill known, simply, as the onion.

Looking at the diagram (Fig. 6) you can see the resemblance. If you've not encountered this float before I hope you'll discover, as I did, just what a useful addition to your tackle box an onion can be, even allowing for the later development of the Dart.

In fact, it is our old friend, the reverse crowquill, with the all-important addition of a small cork body at the lower end of the float.

Its main advantage is that it gives us extra facilities—particularly for casting—that the ordinary and simple reversed crowquills don't.

The extra 'body' enables you to use more lead, increasing casting distance and giving greater control while basically retaining the sensitivity which is such a feature of crowquill fishing.

That increased tackle control is particularly noticeable when fishing deeper sluggish water. And remember none of the quills we have discussed so far are suitable for water in excess of 5 ft. With the onion our maximum depth is increased to 8 ft.

Basically, I suppose, the other crowquills are for small still waters, mostly when conditions are ideal. With the onion we are gradually moving into the family of floats which will cope with bigger waters and rougher conditions. The onion won't cope with the biggest river but there are plenty where it will work a treat. One that comes quickly to mind is the Nene in the reaches above Peterborough. It has served me well there.

The reverse crowquill is no more sensitive than the onion but, to coin a phrase, it's a close-quarters float. The onion gives us much greater casting distance and can be used in water with a certain amount of flow.

One of the first things you'll find about the onion is that a lift bite with it becomes a real cracker. No other float I know gives a more positive lift reaction. The tip fairly looms up out of the water in a way which makes the bite absolutely unmistakable—and, of course, that much easier to hit.

Another thing which at first surprised me about the onion is that, despite its shape, you get little drag or wind resistance. In fact its abilities in this direction are perhaps better than the ordinary reversed quill.

Once again, you will see that the float is fished from the bottom and carries a twist of lead wire just above the ring (see Fig. 6). As with the normal reverse quill it must be exactly the right amount and pre-testing is essential. All the shot—in this case one BB, one No. 4 and two dust—should be pinched on a loop of nylon and lead wire added until the final 'show' is $1\frac{1}{4}$ in., giving a tip of 1 in. when actually fishing.

But the spacing of the shot has changed considerably and this is why. Extra lead has been added to the terminal length, first, and most obviously, to compensate for the addition of a cork body and, secondly, to prevent over-shooting the end tackle on the cast, thus preventing the kind of tangles so common with the ordinary porcupine quill float.

The shotting below the float is self-explanatory and devised to ensure a smooth fall of the bait through the water. The position of shot C as before, is varied for the reason I have already given—to beat shy fish.

Another interesting facility about the onion is the way in which the terminal shot can be varied to beat a head-on wind in a way which could lead to tangles round the float with the ordinary reverse quill. If the headwind is strong, slide shot A down to fish alongside shot B. If the wind is stiff but not too bad, change the positions of the two shots—so that the No. 4 goes 12 in. below the float and the BB 20 in. from the hook.

Once more the diagram shows the bait being fished off the bottom and this—almost without exception—is the way I use it. You can try laying-on with an onion but I wouldn't recommend it, especially when there's even the slightest pull on the water. In these circumstances, it becomes a real jumping onion, pulling under constantly in a way which makes it impossible to tell clearly whether you've got a bite or not.

Another thing which is different about the onion compared with the simple reverse quill is the reason governing the distance of the dust shot which lies between float and rod tip. The distance you are casting is no longer the deciding factor. The thing that counts now is the amount of wind you have to cope with. The stronger the wind the farther the shot is placed from the float ring, although never more than the maximum given in the diagram of 24 in. The closest setting, 4 in., would be justified only in the most gentle breeze.

The onion has one other attribute although it's not one I often use. It can be set to fish as shallow as 2 ft. and yet be cast a fair distance without tangles developing. Anyone who has ever fished this way—shallow and far off—must have found that their end-tackle was prone to tangles in flight. The bulge on the onion holds the float back in the air without impeding the progress of the leads—and so those tangles are eliminated.

To give you an example, picture a canal where you want to fish under the opposite bank where the water is shallow. The onion is just the ticket. Quite apart from giving you freedom from tangles, it is just as efficient a bite indicator as ever.

But the onion does have its restrictions and it would be wrong of me to seem too confident about the variety of its uses. Apart from the restrictions on depth, it should never be used in streamy or turbulent water.

It's fine in all still waters, good in canals and in sluggish rivers. I've already mentioned the Middle Nene and another good example would be for reasonably close-in roach fishing in the Lower Welland.

Strangely enough the onion, especially in view of its usefulness, is something of a tackle shop rarity. In my experience you'll certainly have a job buying one unless you really hunt for them.

The best way to get exactly the right thing, is to make them yourself. All that's needed is a suitable quill, a small cork, an eyelet ring and some silk for whipping it on. One small caution for do-it-yourself onion bashers. Be careful not to fit the cork body too low on the quill or you won't have room for attaching that vital lead wire.

Having told you all I can about the onion, that completes our discussions on the crowquill patterns.

Master these simple quill floats. The more you get the message about them and the more you understand WHY you are using them in a certain way, the more easily you'll understand the complex ideas to follow.

Chapter 3

The Avon Floats

The problem of how best to long-trot a bait through running water—especially water of the more turbulent variety—is one which has come in for endless discussion among anglers.

One of the latest in a long line of bright ideas to arrive on the angling scene as a remedy for our trotting ills was the fluted float. To me it's a nil notion which achieves nothing very special.

My salvation in these conditions for as long as I can remember has been the family of floats known as Avons. There is nothing new to them but don't accuse me of being old-fashioned. I stay faithful to these floats because, for me, they are still the answer to my trotting problems.

I've lost count of the number of match awards these floats have won for me, or for that matter the number of difficult problems they have solved on pleasure outings.

To any young up-and-coming angler I'd say ignore all the ballyhoo about new-fangled ideas for long-trotting. Master the Avon float technique and you'll rarely fail in streamy water.

There's one exception to all this—the day when there's a downstream wind. But don't worry about this just now. We've got an answer to this problem and I'll be telling you about it later.

Having pleaded so strongly for my favourite Avons I'd better tell you what they are and why I like 'em so much. They are, so far as I can discover, named after the Warwick-shire Avon, which I imagine is the water where they were first found to be so effective. Certainly, it happened before my time!

Since those early days, the Avons have gone on to prove their usefulness in streamy waters, big and small, all over the country ... the Severn, Trent, Thames, Tweed, to name just four fairly widespread waters at random.

When I first wrote about these floats in *Angler's Mail* I said they were best made with a crowquill stem which carried a cork body near the thick tip of the float. At the time it was a good combination for in using these materials like this we found that to the general sensitivity of the crowquill cork was adding greater buoyancy at the top—a vital need as I see it for long-trotting, especially in rougher conditions.

The cork, of course, also meant something else when the float was compared with a simple quill. It would carry more lead. These two factors made this the perfect float for the job giving complete control over tackle and bait at all times.

The cork was fighting to keep the tip at the surface while the shot used to give you control over your terminal tackle was trying to pull it down. And while these principles are still most important the Avons—and the Duckers which we are to consider next—have changed for we have been forced to find new materials for making them and, in doing so, have discovered ways of making them fish more efficiently than before.

Like so many of the important developments in fishing it was something of an accident. None of us had any thoughts about changing these floats until we were forced to. And the reason was simple. We suddenly found that there was —and still is—a nationwide shortage of crowquills in the medium and large sizes needed for making these floats correctly, a shortage which is particularly acute with the larger quills.

So bad did things become it became obvious we were going to have to find different materials for making these floats if we were going to be able to continue using them.

And this took time. At first we found we could still, if

we were extremely lucky, obtain some crowquills but, almost without exception, they turned out to be on the small side when it came to using them for the manufacture of Avons and Duckers and all our attempts to continue making the floats with these quills merely ended up with float stems which tended to break on the strike.

At the same time, there were some larger quills about but these turned out to be from sea birds and, as I am sure you will notice immediately if you examine them yourself, you will see that they do not have the same streamlined shape of the crowquill, a shape which, to me, has always been one of the essential advantages of this material for making floats of the type we are discussing. We also found, incidentally, that it was next to impossible to get the cork body to fit properly on these sea bird quills in a way which would make the float give the correct 'show' in the water.

Next we tried that old favourite for some, porcupine quill, but here again there were problems. Because their diameters varied so much the job of fitting the float body to them became a nightmare or just plain impossible.

In the end, I decided that the best way of solving the problem was to dispense with the use of quills altogether and to begin looking for something else which, one hoped, would serve the same purpose.

And the answer we finally came up with was cane, for the stem, and balsa, for the body, both materials which gave us the ability to work to exactly the size we wanted with every float. The stem is shaped so that it is thicker at the tip (see diagrams), thinning out where it passes through the body of the float, and going thinner still in the stem. That, of course, was for the Avon. With the Duckers, the process was almost but not quite reversed, as you will see.

The body is shaped balsa and after being slid on to the cane is glued, the whole thing being painted and thoroughly varnished to make it watertight.

Now all this meant that, for the first time, we could make Avons and Duckers exactly the same size every time—a thing which was impossible with crowquills for the stem and cork for the body.

With these latter materials there was always a variation in the floats, a variation which could often mean that the shot carrying capacities of two floats which seemingly looked exactly the same size could often differ with, say, a medium size Avon, by as much as a AAA shot. In other words, every one of these floats had to be individually shotted beforehand if one was to be able to use them speedily and efficiently.

It should follow that because the new Avons and Duckers made with cane and balsa are capable of being made exactly the same size the shotting capacity of every one of them in each particular size, is precisely the same and their accuracy can be absolutely relied upon. So, apart from solving a problem caused by the shortage of a once vital material, this is our first bonus—a group of floats which can be accurately shotted as a group for the first time.

But, as we came to use the floats made from these new materials more often, we quickly found that there were further gains in terms of their efficiency.

Most important is that we now have much greater control over the buoyancy of the float. With the old Avons and Duckers the cork body *had* to go where it fitted tightest on the quill stem for the float to be fished satisfactorily. The trouble with this, particularly with the Avons, meant that there was all too often a longer antenna or tip above the cork body than there needed to be, a factor which distinctly interfered with the 'show' of the float, the presentation of the bait, and the control of the float.

With the new material—cork and balsa—we can fit the body of the Avon much nearer the tip because we are no longer governed by the diameter of the quills which were used before. And, of course, we can put it in the same place every time and this also means that we can make the tip thicker or thinner at will so that the buoyancy of the float— the relation of tip and stem to body—is perfect.

Another bonus is that the 'show' of the Avons and Duckers now is much prouder in the water than it was before without in any way interfering with the sensitivity of the tackle, an advance of the greatest usefulness.

The fact, too, that we are now able to exactly control the diameter of the float stem also helps give us better control when actually fishing especially in fast water. The old style Avon, however well you fished it, had a nasty habit of tending to rise up in the water on checking, a thing which could, of course, disturb the bait in such a way that it could cost you a bite. The new cane and balsa job doesn't have this habit to the same degree, if at all.

Size for size, the new Avons and Duckers have similar shot carrying capacities to the old ones.

For the benefit of readers who wish to make their own Avon floats, these are the dimensions I work to and the shot carrying capacities in each case.

$5\frac{1}{2}$ in. stem, $1\frac{1}{4}$ in. long body, 3BB;
6 in. stem, $1\frac{1}{2}$ in. body, 4BB;
$6\frac{1}{2}$ in. stem, $1\frac{7}{8}$ in. body, 5BB;
7 in. stem, $2\frac{1}{4}$ in. body, 6BB;
$6\frac{1}{2}$ in. stem, $2\frac{1}{2}$ in. body, 2 swan;
7 in. stem, 3 in. body, $2\frac{1}{2}$ swan;
$7\frac{1}{2}$ in. stem, $3\frac{1}{2}$ in. body, 3 swan.

So much then for the changes there have been in these floats since I first wrote about them. Let's look now at the job of fishing them and to do this I shall be taking you through several sizes of Avon first so that you can see how really versatile they are.

Let's discuss first the smallest model I use (see Fig. 7).

This float would be ideal for long-trotting maggots or caster baits in rivers like the Trent where the swim is strong flowing, perhaps a bit turbulent, and the wind is upstream.

I say it's a good maggot or caster float because I don't think it necessary to use an excessive amount of lead with these baits and it follows that only a smallish Avon will permit this.

This particular Avon, as the diagram should tell you, is fixed at the top with a valve-rubber, the line running through

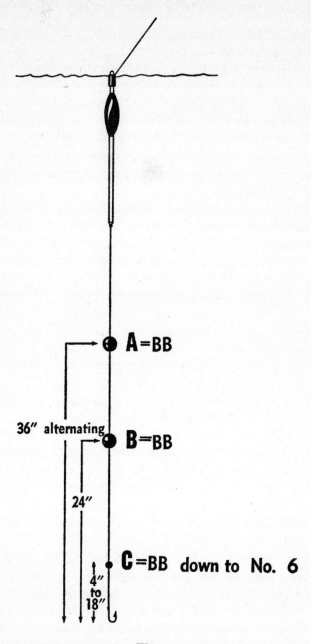

Fig. 7

the bottom ring to the terminal tackle.

The valve-rubber should be fixed a quarter-inch from the tip of the float if conditions permit it to be easily seen. If they don't lower it a fraction, though never much more than half an inch from the tip. If it can't be seen at half an inch you need to switch to a bigger Avon.

The shotting is designed to get the bait down quickly so that it's in the likeliest area for fish as soon as possible in the swim—the bottom or somewhere near it. And the pattern shown is the one I use most.

Shot A is the one used to get things down quickly and you can see it's alternating. This means that where the water is deeper (you could afford to fish up to 9 ft. with this size Avon) you can afford to put shot A nearer the hook. It should never be *farther* than 3 ft. from the hook. Depth and the force of the stream are the deciding factors here. The deeper the swim, the stronger the current, the nearer shot A goes to the hook, on some occasions down so far until it is actually grouped with shot B.

The position of this shot—24 in. from the hook—is unvarying. Its main job is to prevent tangles on casting.

Shot C is your tell-tale for bites. Many times when long-trotting you will, like me, have retrieved the tackle to find the maggots have been pulped. And yet you've seen no bite. That's because shot C, at 18 in. from the hook, was too far away for positive registration. The fish had too much freedom to mouth the bait. To combat this merely move shot C nearer the hook, remembering that the nearer you take it the more likely it is with an Avon that a bite will be shown by a 'lift'.

In our diagram, the bait is being fished off the bottom—the most usual but not the only style. An alternative is to let the bait drag on the bottom by shifting the float up the line, though never so far that shot C is allowed to touch bottom. That would render the entire rig useless.

For laying-on all but the very biggest Avons are perfect. That terrific buoyancy at the tip explains this. When the tackle is being fished this way the float holds the surface

Billy displays nearly 200 lb. of carp taken in one day's fishing on the River Ebro in Spain. To get them he used his famous sliding porcupine quill float.

Get together of Britain's two most famous anglers ... Billy (foreground) and Richard Walker, fishing here from a boat at Grafham water.

Billy Lane with the signs of his match fishing success. Among the trophies, which are only part of the pots he has won, is the World Championship cup. So valuable was this little display the picture was taken at the police station in Billy's home city, Coventry, because that was considered the safest place.

steadily. All you have to do to lay-on is shift the float up the line the appropriate distance and move shots A and B the same distance.

Float legering, while fine with some of the Avons as you will discover, is not a good idea with this smaller version.

So much then for the Avon which will cope with the small to medium rivers. What about those which will cope with bigger rivers.

At its largest, with a stem of nine inches and a body of three, the Avon is really heavy gear.

But on the Severn between Bridgnorth and Worcester—some of the toughest water I know where it's really deep and heavy pulling—the big Avon and the shot it can carry is the equaliser you need to catch the fish.

Personally, I know of no 'bigger' water than this one for nowhere else do I go this big or heavy with float tackle.

But before going on to discuss the bigger Avons in detail, I'd like to make a general point about these floats.

At all times when using Avons, the terminal tackle must precede the float through the swim. To many this may seem obvious. I make the point simply for the benefit of those who are trying the Avon floats for the first time.

To get this correct flow of tackle cast slightly upstream from the point where your swim begins—and I do mean slightly. Hold your rod high in the air until the float has cocked and begun its journey down the swim. Bring your rod down holding it pointing slightly downstream, a position you will retain throughout the swimming down. By completing these motions—and especially by making sure your line is lying straight to the float when the rod is high—you will ensure the terminal tackle is travelling correctly.

It is most important that you don't make any check on the float while it is travelling down the swim. With tackle of this weight, jerky movements will alarm the fish considerably. The best thing when in doubt is to lift the rod slightly and you will see it taking up the line between rod tip and the float.

By watching the line you can release the tension on the

tackle before the pull you are creating has reached the float and caused one of those jerks.

If this still doesn't satisfy you, let the tackle complete its run, retrieve, and try again rather than cause any jerks in the water being fished.

And now for those bigger Avon patterns. We switch to them because the water is deeper, stronger flowing, more turbulent, and because the wind—remember it's upstream when you use these Avons—is stronger.

Any one of these reasons is justification enough to scale up the size of the float. But only when all of them are operative should you use the biggest Avon.

Let's put the spotlight now on a medium Avon—the next size up from the small version we have just discussed. This float would be used in a river with a medium-strong flow with possibly some turbulence in the water and a stiffish breeze.

I've used it a lot in the Upper Great Ouse in the Newport Pagnell reaches and again on the Thames.

This—and the bigger Avons—are the heaviest floats we have used so far. They are, as I hope you will see, living proof that fishing heavy is the most natural thing in the world when conditions dictate it.

Anglers generally seem frightened of heavy shotting and I've suffered many a tease for my heavy tactics. The difference between these folk and me is that I've learned to understand that despite those big shots, if the tackle is balanced correctly the only weight the fish feel is the last tell-tale shot on the line.

Northern matchmen seem particularly prone to offer me this kind of wigging, being convinced that one must always fish light. They are welcome to their theories. I know I am right and they can please themselves whether they accept my advice or ignore it.

They are wrong because they are insisting that the water should accept the tackle they want to inflict on it when the equation should be the other way round—the water (and the conditions) should dictate the tackle used.

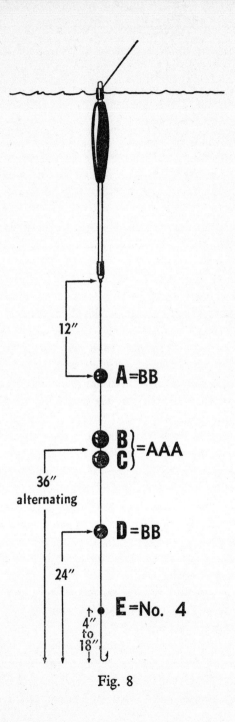

Fig. 8

Certainly, I'd back myself to win hands down with my heavy gear against light in the kind of water we are discussing now.

But I digress. Let's get back to that medium Avon (Fig. 8). As you can see it carries a fair amount of shot, two AAA, two BB and one No. 4.

Its usefulness is best proved by a story about a match I fished in the Great Ouse at Milton Ernest when it was a roughish sort of day. I won with 34 lb. of roach—note that, roach—nearly 15 lb. more than my nearest rival could muster. To do it I fished running water along the far bank, the weight of the tackle giving me easy casting and tight control once the trot began.

This float—the stem is about seven inches long, the balsa about two inches—is fixed with two valve rubbers to make for easy changes, either up or down in size.

The shotting, because of the distance cast, is designed mainly to keep the terminal tackle clear of the float on casting, a thing which becomes more and more important as you step up the weight with Avon floats.

The first shot A (a BB) is always 12 in. below the float. It's a tell-tale I set after first plumbing the depth. However much I vary the depth while fishing I know that 12 in. above this shot was my original reading. It follows, too, that I can tell at a glance if my float has slipped on the line.

The AAAs lettered B and C are the bulk shot which speed the tackle down into the water and their position varies between 36 in. and less from the hook according to the pull of the stream. The greater it is, the lower they go, even to the extent of being grouped with shot D which is 24 in. from the hook.

But generally they remain separated from shot D, whose basic purpose is to guard against back tangles with float and terminal gear on casting.

The last shot, E, is fairly light—a No. 4. It's the only one taking fish feel and it's so light compared to the others because, on the Great Ouse, and rivers like it, you tend to get a pretty snaggy weed cover on the bottom. A light shot here allows the bait to rise easily over those weeds.

This shot, too, is an alternator for reasons we have discussed before—for shy bites it is moved nearer the hook. Actually you will find it rarely needs moving lower than 18 in. with this heavy tackle for generally the bites are really strong.

Once again the diagram shows the bait being fished off the bottom. The float can, however, be adjusted to let the bait drag the bed but it must not be moved so high that shot E is allowed to touch.

Also possible with this rig is laying-on and float-legering.

To lay-on work to my previous formula, raising the float and shots A, B and C one extra foot up the line for every four feet of depth. Eliminate shot E and put shot D 18 in. from the hook.

To float-leger, fit a $\frac{1}{8}$ oz. Hillman anti-kink lead on the line above shot D (eliminate shot E again), going a little bigger with the Hillman lead if the flow requires it. Be more generous when moving the float and the rest of the shot up the line—say 18 in. for every four feet of water.

You would only resort to this form of float-legering when you found the pull of the water was too great to permit normal laying-on and that's often in a bream water where, despite the flow, you've found the fish are only interested in a bait really nailed to the bottom.

Heavy gear like this means stronger lines. It's no good using 2 lb. nylon with the bigger Avons. You'll break up. Line between $3\frac{1}{2}$ lb. and $4\frac{1}{2}$ lb. is ideal, the latter being the heaviest I would consider it necessary to go.

From medium Avons we move now, finally, to the biggest of this family, the floats I would use in the strongest water. And of those I fish regularly I would cite the River Severn between Bridgnorth and Stourport as a typical example.

This is a rough old piece of river which really needs the weight these big Avons give you. But it's not the only place I would use one.

Another water with swims which could easily justify this kind of tackle is that specimen hunter's dream, the Hampshire Avon. And, friends, have there been some fancy tackles suggested for that place!

I've seen some fabulous monstrosities—none of which could hold a candle to the orthodox version of a big Avon, with the proviso that the chosen swim was free of obstructions on the bottom. Given a clear swim these Avons are THE tackle boss in the famous Hampshire river.

And even in the weediest water there, it's still an Avon float you want. I found this out by experience on an entirely different river—the Windrush at Whitney in Oxfordshire. Unknown to me at the time this is rather like a Hampshire Avon in miniature, fast-flowing and with huge clumps of streamer weed.

At first I tried a heavyish Avon float tackle but the leads constantly tangled in the weeds. The answer? I found that by switching to a smaller Avon float—like the one I talked about earlier—it was easily possible to trot the river efficiently without a single tangle, provided that all the weight except the final shot was placed directly under the float.

This piece of information lodged firmly in my mind and when I later went to the Hampshire Avon I found all the same things to be true. The bigger Avon was just fine with a clear bottom. Where there were weeds I simply did a Windrush and switched to a smaller Avon to get complete control of my tackle.

My reservations about the Hampshire Avon, incidentally, offer a good yardstick about when to decide to go heavier with an Avon float. Wherever there is excessive weed growth you want to avoid lead in any quantity on the terminal length.

So the thing to remember when thinking about heavy Avon tackle for heavy water is that you must have a clear run down the swim.

The float fixture is as before—two valve rubbers—but when I want to go really heavy with an Avon the shotting pattern changes (see Fig. 9).

We've got swan shot on the line now but the rig will fish swims as shallow as four feet and as deep as ten. The

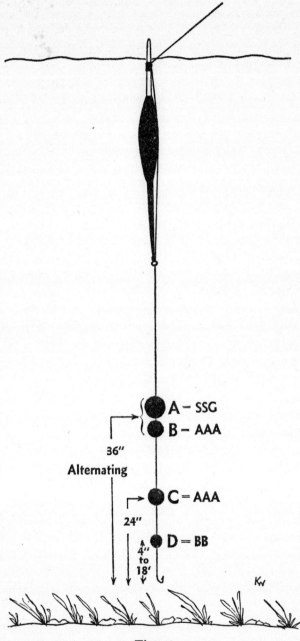

Fig. 9

only deciding factor now—apart from a downstream wind which would rule out an Avon anyway—is the power of the flow. With leads like this on, no other wind, not even a gale, will worry you.

With this powerful flow—and remember it can be stronger in 4 ft. of water than at greater depths—the idea is to get the bait down quickly so that it's among the fish as long as possible on the swim down. That's the job of shots A and B. Again the flow decides where they go. The stronger it is the nearer the hook they go, sometimes, although this is rare, lumped together with shot C.

In case this appals you, don't worry—for still the only shot the fish will feel is shot D and that is only a BB, a mere midget in these kind of conditions. And fish in this heavy water are not likely to be fickle feeders. If they are going to have a go they'll take with a bang and bites will be unmistakable.

Shot C is your guard against tangles and while I have said that it's possible conditions will lead you to bulk A, B and C together, it is certainly true to say that the farther you can manage to keep A and B from C the less likely you are to develop tangles round the float.

To give you another indication of the very real power of water I'm talking about, you will have noticed the tackle is being fished off the bottom—and that's the only way you could fish it! To get any bait fixed to the bottom in such conditions you'd be forced to revert to straightforward legering. Laying-on would be out of the question.

You could just get away with bumping a bait along the bottom, but only by making sure that shot D never touched.

You wouldn't get away with float legering with this float because it's too big. The float would be constantly dithering in a way which would make bites impossible to spot.

There is one other wrinkle you can use with this big float for fishing with cereal baits like paste and crust for chub in winter—and that's to get rid of shot D. By removing this you will achieve better presentation of these baits. But don't do it in any other circumstances.

Now the tackle in our diagram is heavy—but not the heaviest. There are occasions when you will want even more weight than this and once again it's the Avon that comes to the rescue.

The float I'm thinking about will be fished with three swans at point AB with an AAA at point C. Its stem will be no longer but its body will be fatter—the balance needed for the extra weight being provided by a bigger diameter body.

To be well equipped Avonwise I'd recommend you to have a reasonable selection in your wallet—with stems ranging from $5\frac{1}{2}$ to $7\frac{1}{2}$ inches and each stem having two or three variations in the diameter of the body. A selection like this will greatly increase your versatility with the floats.

Before summing up on Avons, I'd like to emphasise again that you don't need to worry about weight. The only thing to worry about is that the weight you do use is exactly counter-balanced by the float and that in achieving the balance you should ensure that the smallest unit of weight is nearest the hook.

The bath-room test I mentioned earlier for the reverse crowquill and onion floats is just the job for sorting this problem out.

Now let me recap briefly about Avons NEVER—and it's the most important consideration of all—use an Avon with a downstream wind. DON'T use them in still water. NEVER, with the larger sizes, waste your time trying to lay-on. NEVER at any time allow the bottom shot on the tackle to touch bottom while trotting. NEVER use them with a line lighter than $3\frac{1}{2}$ lb. breaking strain. DON'T FORGET you are using these floats to beat the wind on casting and the current's strength when long trotting. And NEVER attempt to fish an Avon in water that is deeper than the length of your rod.

Chapter 4

The Duckers

Now while the Avon floats we have just been discussing are tremendously useful in running water there is, as I have already mentioned, one big limiting factor with them ... they are no good at all when the wind is blowing downsteam.

The answer to this problem is simply to switch to another family of floats—closely related to the Avon—which will solve this difficulty for you and others as well. I am referring to the floats that anglers in the Midlands have always called Duckers.

How the name originated is something I don't know but it goes back as long as I can remember. I've used 'em for years and I expect to go on using Duckers for many more to come. In certain circumstances there is nothing to touch them.

I am particularly devoted to one variety—as you will discover in detail later—for it brought me my best ever result in the National Championship.

To look at, Duckers are like Avons with the big exception that the body is now mounted near the bottom of the stem.

The main object of these floats is to beat wind—particularly the downstream variety—and if you look at the diagrams you'll see that it's done by burying the line in a similar way to that used with the reverse crowquill and the onion floats.

The beauty of the Ducker is that unlike the Avon, which would only be used in running water, the Ducker is a float for still *and* running water. It is, in fact, one of the most useful floats there is.

It is also one of only four types of float I ever use which has the body at the lower end of the stem. One is the onion, which in effect is a Ducker on a reversed quill stem. The others, to be described later, are zoomers and sliding antennas.

These Duckers have the cane stem upwards and the body low down, a feature which gives the Ducker its wind cheating ability giving you virtually automatic sinking of the line, hastened, except with the larger floats, by the addition of a shot between rod and float. And in still and sluggish waters this back shot is often not needed even with the lighter Duckers.

Even when the line is slack the Ducker will trot down the swim evenly giving you natural bait presentation. With the Avons, you recall, great care had to be taken to keep the rod constantly in touch with the float so that the bait preceded it down the swim. With a downstream wind the Ducker will permit you to trot the bait down a smooth swim at the natural speed of the water. An Avon used in the same conditions would speed on ahead of the terminal tackle and ruin bite detection.

In other words, the Ducker doesn't have to be bullied to be kept in its proper place. This, and its ability to beat the wind, are its greatest assets.

Like the Avons there's a whole range of Duckers. Obviously, the bigger boys are for the worst conditions. To try and set you off right on a Ducker kick it's best, I think, if we talk about using them in their smallest form first.

Then, if the Ducker is new to you, you'll be able to approach the larger sizes with their heavy shotting with less apprehension.

The float is attached to the line by the eyelet ring only by a method we've already talked about—a series of loops through the ring.

In its smallest form, the shotting, as you'll see from the diagram (Fig. 10)—is comparatively light, consisting of not

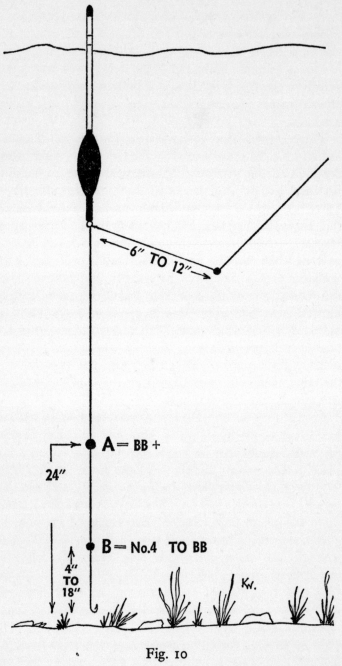

Fig. 10

more than the two BB shown below the float. I asked our artist not to label the shot above the float because this can vary so much.

At most it would be a No. 6 and this would be in sluggish water, the fastest in which you would use this size of Ducker. At its smallest it would be a dust shot and then the downstream wind and the flow would be at a minimum. The formula for the distance of this shot I have mentioned before —the greater the flow and the stronger wind the farther it goes from the float ring, up to a maximum of 12 in.

Downstairs, the shot pattern is simple. At point A a single BB or possibly one AAA—but no more with this size of Ducker—to get the bait down. And at point B the usual tell-tale shot for bites which alternate according to the strength of the takes.

Once again you can allow the bait to trail bottom so long as shot B never touches bottom. But laying-on is useless with Duckers unless the water is virtually static. If conditions are right, move the float up the line the required depth —one foot for every four feet of depth—and lay shot B only on the bottom.

As the Ducker is a fixed float you are limited to the depth of water you can use it in. A comfortable yardstick to use is to treat the maximum as a foot less than the length of your rod. These smaller Duckers are suitable for lakes, ponds, canals and rivers where the flow and the downstream wind is not excessive.

There are heavier Duckers and these are the sort that are mostly a straightforward replacement for Avons in running water where there is a downstream wind. The biggest— 7 in. long with a balsa body $3\frac{1}{2}$ in. long—would be used in rivers with the strongest flow you can think of and the roughest downstream wind possible. They'd also be used in still water when I've got a gale blowing straight in my face.

With these we've reached a similar stage to that we came to when discussing the bigger Avons. If these big Duckers won't do what you want then legering is your only alternative.

To give you some idea just how good I've found these heavier Duckers let me say that I won a match in the Trent with one when everybody who watched said I was potty to even think of putting it on. There were 600 in the match and I won with a stone of fish—twice my nearest rival's weight.

Even more spectacular for me was the year when Coventry began their now famous victory march in the National Championship in the River Witham. In this match I used the heaviest Ducker of all to get 19 lb. of bream and third individual place—my best-ever National performance. People refused to believe I had used such heavy gear despite the fact that the Witham was pulling stronger than anyone had ever seen it go.

Let's have a detailed look now at these bigger members of the Ducker family. They're heavy all right—but not, in my opinion, as crude as the alternative of legering. The smallest of them (Fig. 11) is the one I used to win the Trent match I mentioned.

I was fishing for the same fairly small sample of roach we find there today but I never missed a bite from those little beauties with this comparatively heavy rig.

It was a howling day with a downstream wind almost strong enough to blow you off your basket. I discovered at the end of it that I'd been one of only a few competitors who had been able to get a float on the water successfully. The rest had reverted to last-ditch legering—or packed up!

Look first at the shotting (see Fig. 11 again). The bulk shot at Point A—three AAAs on this day—is pretty heavy, especially in the Trent. But I wouldn't have hesitated to add more had conditions got worse still.

The swim was about ten feet deep so that allowed me to put these bulk shot at the nearest permissible point to the hook—four feet away. If it had been less they would have gone higher—a rule to remember when considering this float.

Shot B is my anti-tangle shot and as the wind was so strong I used a fourth AAA. Here again you will notice this

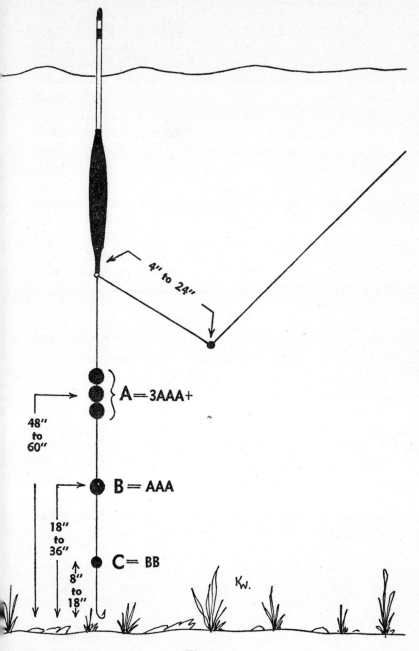

4" to 24"

A = 3AAA+

48"
to
60"

B = AAA

18"
to
36"

C = BB

8"
to
18"

K.W.

Fig. 11

is an alternating shot and again the depth decides it. If the bulk shot are at five feet, shot B is at three feet. If the bulk go on at four feet then B comes down to 18 inches.

Shot C—a BB—was my tell-tale for bites and it's this size because of the strong flow. It is, as I have emphasised before, the only shot the fish feel.

The line-sinking shot above the float was set at the maximum 24 inches. Had the wind been less it would have been nearer the float ring.

But, despite the dreadful conditions, I was able to get my bait out with ease, see bites clearly and catch a stone of fish.

The argument before the match was: 'He'll never catch fish in the Trent with all that weight on.' But I did, because for me there was never any argument. I had learned, as I hope you will, the point I have made again and again— that if the float is big enough to exactly counter-balance the weight of the shot there is nothing to worry about.

The Trent is not the only place where such a float could succeed. There are plenty of other rivers where you'd use it to beat such conditions—a strong flow and a strong downstream wind is all you need for their selection to become automatic. It will also work in still water when the wind is severe to gale-force.

Yet even with this Ducker there comes a stage when conditions are deteriorating so much that it becomes impossible to trot it down the swim efficiently. It keeps going under to give you false bites.

When this happens all you have to do is go heavier! Put on a Ducker with a bigger body still, the float in the next diagram (Fig. 12).

This fat-bodied Ducker would trot the worst part of the Severn in a howling downstream gale giving you complete control over your tackle. It was this very float which did me so well in that Witham National I mentioned.

The first thing you should notice about this, the biggest of the Duckers, is that the shot above the float has disappeared. Let's face it, there's no difficulty sinking the line

Billy demonstrates the sliding antenna technique (right) to French-
man Robert Tesse (left) three times World Champion in the shadow
of the famous Chateau Richelieu at Les Andelys. Robert is now a
keen convert to the technique.

Renowned for his patience with the younger angler, Billy is seen here on the Thames at Tadpole. On this occasion he had spent nearly six hours trying to catch a barbel and the moment he hooked it he passed his rod to the youngster in the picture so that he could have the pleasure of landing it.

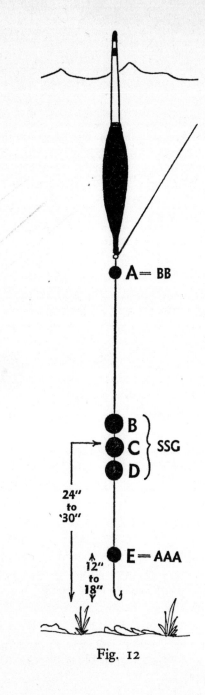

Fig. 12

when we've got three swan shot, one AAA and one BB under the float.

Shot A—you've seen one of those before by now, too— is a tell-tale which lets me know whether my float has slipped on the line, a tendency which is increased with this heavier tackle.

The depth of the water decides where the bulk swans go —30 inches in fairly shallow stuff, 24 inches in deep water. The shot the fish feel this time is an AAA (shot E) so you can tell how hard the water had to be going to justify this kind of thing. But it is justified. That's the important thing to realise.

On this Witham day I was fighting a particularly strong current. The wind wasn't much to worry about but the river really was pulling faster than anyone had ever known. Yet I was able to cast clean across the Witham and trot down along the far bank with complete control. I got 19 lb. of fish and I'm certain it wouldn't have been half that amount had I been legering.

With bread baits another adjustment is necessary. Shot E should be moved up to join the bulk shot, leaving a 24 in. tail. I find the tackle works better with this pattern and that it's particularly useful when the bed of the swim is uneven or weedy.

Ideally, this heaviest of all Duckers should be used for long-trotting. Certainly laying-on should never be attempted with it, although you can set the float higher to allow the bait to drag bottom with the usual reservation that Shot E mustn't touch.

As with Avons, if you are really going to have a go with Duckers you need to stock up on sizes. You want floats with stems from 4 in. to 7 in. The bodies should vary, too, in length and diameter for each size of stem.

For while this can be heavy fishing, you will still find that the exactness of light float-fishing is necessary in terms of balance. You need to be as versatile as possible with the amount of shot and only a reasonably wide selection of floats can give you that.

Having told you two cautionary tales about Duckers, I wouldn't like you to think that the rivers mentioned are the only ones where they can be successfully employed. Duckers will work anywhere, in any river, canal, lake or pond.

It's just a matter of matching the size of float to the prevailing water and weather conditions.

For the benefit of readers who wish to make their own Ducker floats, these are the dimensions I work to and the shot carrying capacities in each case:

4 in. stem, $1\frac{1}{4}$ in. long body, 3 BB
$4\frac{1}{2}$ in. stem, $1\frac{1}{2}$ in. body, 4 BB
5 in. stem, $1\frac{3}{4}$ in. body, 5 BB
$5\frac{1}{2}$ in. stem, 2 in. body, 6 BB
6 in. stem, $2\frac{1}{2}$ in. body, 2 swan
$6\frac{1}{2}$ in. stem, 3 in. body, $2\frac{1}{2}$ swan
7 in. stem, $3\frac{1}{2}$ in. body, 3 swan

Chapter 5

The sliding antenna and stop knots

Now I am going to tell you to get knotted! Again with good reason ... to help you improve your float fishing even further. I am, of course, referring to a particular knot, one which seems to have perplexed more anglers than any other. It's the stop knot I use for sliding floats, the next important family of floats I want to discuss. But before I go into detail about them it's essential you learn how to tie the knot which is used as a stopper with them. It has been dealt with before in the angling press but never in a way which satisfied me.

The result has been a puzzle for many who have tried to tie what is basically an extremely simple knot. And if you find this hard to believe let me tell you here and now that I couldn't possibly count the thousands of times I've had to demonstrate this knot in recent years ... sure proof, I think you'll agree, that this small but vital subject has been fogbound for far too long.

Thanks to our diagrams, I hope you'll find the final end to this knotty problem. They are the finest I have seen—they really explain the knot in the simplest possible way.

It may sound as though I am taking this all a bit too seriously but if the diagrams and instructions are understood as easily as I think they will be, then I shall literally be relieved of thousands more demonstrations of this knot. And frankly, I can do with the time that would be saved.

So, first look at the diagrams (Figs. 13, 14 and 15) carefully and then have a bash yourself. Take a piece of nylon

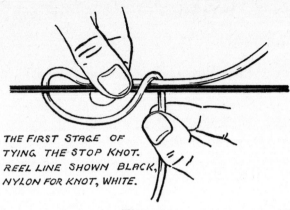

THE FIRST STAGE OF
TYING THE STOP KNOT.
REEL LINE SHOWN BLACK,
NYLON FOR KNOT, WHITE.

Fig. 13

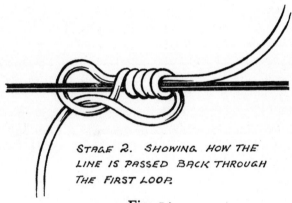

STAGE 2. SHOWING HOW THE
LINE IS PASSED BACK THROUGH
THE FIRST LOOP.

Fig. 14

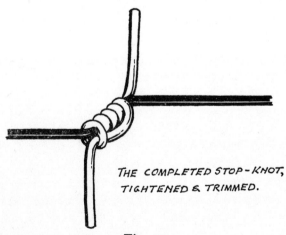

THE COMPLETED STOP-KNOT,
TIGHTENED & TRIMMED.

Fig. 15

line—about six inches is just right—and form it into a U-loop. Lay this alongside the reel line and then pull one end over to form a loop, the position in the first of the three diagrams.

The next step is simply to wind this end over the reel line four or five times and then thread it through the loop that is left (second diagram). By pulling the two ends of the piece of nylon tight you should end up with the knot in diagram 3. Simple, isn't it?'

Now I suggested you use a piece of nylon six inches long for this job—and for an extremely important reason. A knot with short ends would stop a sliding float moving from its required position on the line. But what a snag you'd find it on the cast as, one after the other, it caught like a brake on every ring on your rod.

By having longer ends this difficulty is completely eliminated. For the smallest sliding floats I'd trim the ends to not less than 1 in.; for the bigger ones, 2 in.

Now to correct another misapprehension about this knot which I've read several times in the past ... namely that the knot shouldn't be pulled too tight or it will kink the line. If you've tied it right, this is nonsense!

Believe me, that knot wants to be as tight on the reel line as you can get it, especially with the bigger floats. When the reel line is slack, it should be virtually impossible to move the knot.

Hold the reel line tight and the knot will move easily up and down it. So don't be scared. Pull that knot tight and then carry out this test as a double check. After a few times you'll do all this automatically.

Let's go on now to look at the whys and wherefores of the sliding float and what it achieves.

To explain this best I don't think I could do better than ask you to think back over all the floats mentioned in this book so far and ask what, if anything, was the limiting factor about all of them.

The answer—I hope without my telling you—was the depth of the water. All the floats talked about so far were fixed floats of one kind or another. And with rod lengths being what they are, this pretty well ruled them out in any water over 13 ft. deep.

For many, I imagine, the answer to this would be to switch to legering. On certain occasions this could be the correct thing to do. On many others, in my opinion, it wouldn't. For as I've maintained before there are more times than most anglers realise when float tackle is always better than the leger ... and the sliding float is your deep water answer.

With a stop knot to run through your rod rings it's obvious you can fish any depth you like with these floats, which, fished correctly, are infinitely more sensitive than most legers.

But as I quickly discovered when I first began detailed experiments with sliders, there are other advantages almost as great. Because of the size of the float and the shot they can carry, they enable a bait to be fished deep, at long distances, both on and off the bottom.

With the sliding antennas, which are fixed at the bottom only, they enable the line to be buried completely in a way which beats the wind and the surface drag.

Compared to legering, casting is much less effort and—a point which should appeal to matchmen—much less time is taken in getting the tackle set in the water ready to signal bites—which, incidentally, present no more resistance to a taking fish than would a simple crowquill.

The water *needn't* be deeper than your rod before you resort to slider fishing. With a fixed float, there always comes a time when the depth gets critical in terms of the length of your rod. Not only is casting difficult when you reach this stretch point but you commonly find the float being tangled up with the top ring on the retrieve.

The slider can come to your rescue here for more comfortable and efficient fishing. For instance if I was using a 12 ft. rod and the water was 10 ft., I'd consider a slider rather than struggle on with a fixed float. Nevertheless, there are limits and in my experience I would say don't use a slider at depths of *less* than 8 ft.

Though it's more than a decade since I finalised my experiments with sliding floats, today I am more than ever convinced that this principle, once established, was one of the greatest single breakthroughs in the history of float fishing.

It opened up whole new horizons for all anglers. In all honesty I find myself incapable of imagining any new development in float fishing which will achieve so much in one fell blow as the slider did.

It certainly revolutionised my fishing and what's more put me in the match prize money many more times than I might have been.

And now for the sliders themselves, floats which many anglers still seem to have difficulty in understanding. And yet the technique is not only useful but extremely simple ... given a little thought and practise.

Perhaps the best way of putting the message across to you is to tell you something of the early days of the sliders and how they came to be perfected.

Almost inevitably it was the drive of matchmen wanting to extend their techniques that led to it all, Coventry matchmen in particular.

Their first research, as I recall it, came in the months which led up to the 1955 National Championship, due to be fished that year in Somerset in the Huntspill River and the King's Sedgemoor Drain.

None of us were keen on legering for the bream there so you can imagine how excited we were when one of our 'spies' returned from Somerset with the news that the locals were getting results with the bream with a form of sliding float.

Within days we'd obtained some of these floats. They were fixed to the line top and bottom by two rings only slightly smaller than the normal pattern with two valve rubbers threaded on between the rings to act as a kind of brake.

To me, the float was crude but it worked—though not very efficiently. When I say this I don't mean to knock my still unknown Somerset friends for they were at least having a go at a difficult problem. Their efforts were certainly the spur which drove me on to experiment.

There were two big troubles with this early slider—it didn't always slide into position properly and it offered enormous resistance on the strike. The Coventry team, including yours truly, liked the idea but not the way it was done. Furious experiments began to try and improve on the float with the idea of beating the Somerset locals at their own game.

After several weeks the best we'd come up with was a porcupine quill with two rings at top and bottom, offset on opposite sides of the float. This, too, worked after a fashion but, like the original from Somerset, it was like hitting a brick on the strike.

Time slipped by quickly and, reluctantly, we decided the idea wasn't good enough yet to justify pinning our faith on it in the National. Instead we used duckers to come second in the match, Coventry's best-ever result up to that time and one we were far from ashamed of for the winners, Sheffield Amalgamated, set up a team weight record for the event that stands to this day.

The sliding float idea was temporarily forgotten—but not by me. I was convinced there were great possibilities so I continued to experiment. And the first thing I did was to forget about porcupine quills. I had already developed the resistance I mentioned earlier to porcupine quills for float making but as you'll discover, while I found my first answer to the slider problem elsewhere, I later returned to the 'porcy' for a different but equally useful reason.

Having done so well with Duckers at the National I decided that this shape might be the answer. After many experiments I finally perfected the sliding antenna.

The big problem was always the accurate stopping of the float at the required depth. I had heard of valve rubbers and even matchsticks being used but I wasn't keen. I felt a knot of some kind was the best answer and the result was the nylon hitch I told you about earlier.

It wasn't the biggest breakthrough—that was reserved for

a decision to fix the float at the bottom end only and with a tiny ring. I can't remember exactly how it dawned on me but I do recall that the moment I thought of it I felt like saying 'Hey presto!'

Making those first rings—they had and still have a diameter of 0.015 inch (i.e. 15/1000ths of an inch)—had my family in stitches. First I borrowed a needle from the wife's sewing box and fixed it in a vice. Then I made the ring by winding 20 lb. alastacum wire tightly around the needle.

It seemed a crazy, footling thing to do but it worked. Incidentally, I tried smaller gauge wire but it was no good. It wouldn't stay in place.

While all this was going on I was also experimenting with materials. I finally chose cane for the stem and balsa for the body. Correctly shotted the float gave three different positive settings, all of which told me that the sequence of events was going the way I wanted it.

Considerably elated, I was still uncertain. As a match angler I needed to succeed with the new idea in the testing conditions of a contest before I could really convince myself that all had gone as well as I had thought.

The first match in which I tried the newborn slider was a Coventry A.A. contest fished by more than 400 on the North Bank of the River Nene. I didn't win—but I was still over the moon for I came second with more than 22 lb. of bream and the winner had only just pipped me by 5 drams!

That was all I needed. I not only knew the float would work but that it was also capable of winning matches. From then on I fished it with all the confidence in the world, winning many matches and being highly placed in many more.

That float was like a live thing to me in that Nene match. I can remember its every movement as if it was some kind of long distance puppet doing just what I wanted it to. First it would lay flat on hitting the water. Next it would spring up and settle to its first setting. The bulk shot had drawn the stop knot to the float rings. Then finally, as the bottom tell-tale went down, the float settled just a little bit farther into the water.

Seconds later it vanished as the first bream took hold. Nothing like a good fish with the first cast of a match!

Even then I remember thinking that this first fish might have been a fluke. I was still on edge when I re-cast. But not after I had netted six of 'em. I was on top of the world and on this particular occasion didn't care a damn whether I won the match or not. The confidence I got from the slider that day has never left me.

Having, I hope, persuaded any doubters about the true merits of the slider, let's now get down to fishing with them ... and first the sliding antenna. These floats come in various sizes to enable more or less lead to be used. The smallest—and I wouldn't go any smaller—will take the equivalent of one swan shot. The biggest will take at least four swans, possibly a bit more.

Whenever possible the lightest float is used. Extra weight is employed for two reasons—to aid casting in strong winds and to speed the descent of the bait in particularly deep water.

The stem is made of cane, the body of balsa wood and each float has one ring at the bottom end, 0.015 of an inch in diameter.

The first thing to do when tackling-up with this rig is to tie on that sliding knot I made such a fuss about. Don't forget, make it as tight as you can.

Now throughout this book I've presumed that like any good fishermen, one of the first things you'd do in your angling day would be to plumb the depth. It can be a tricky operation but it's a most necessary one and this is perhaps as good a time as any to emphasise it. It's a vital step in fishing deep water, though luckily the chore will rarely prove easier, or more accurate, than it will when you are using a sliding float. But there are differences to plumbing with the fixed float and you should note them.

Estimate your depth and set the stop-knot tight on the line. Cast in with the plummet and wait to see if the slider shows. If it doesn't, your stop wants moving farther up the line. When the float does appear is when you have to watch it carefully for it's most important with sliding floats that you are dead accurate.

I always plumb with the shot already on the line (mainly to save time in competition conditions) and I seek to get the 'show' of tip I think is right for the float. With the smallest antenna this will be just over half an inch or so, with the biggest anything up to 2 in. if the weather is rough.

Getting this correct 'show' signifies that all the shot are off the bottom. It's then only necessary to remove the plummet and move the stop-knot a little bit nearer the hook and you have the whole rig fishing perfectly.

One last point on this stage of the operation. You will see from the diagram (Fig. 16) that we have shown the stop-knot some distance above the float. This has only been done to make sure you put it in the right place! Obviously when the tackle is being fished that knot is tight against the float ring which, again for reference purposes, has not been drawn as small as it really is.

Next the shotting ... and this, too, must be just right. I emphasise this because it's yet another bogey, it seems, for newcomers to the sliding float—they're always getting tangles round the float, they tell me. In most cases this is because they have not shotted the terminal tackle correctly.

Let's take a detailed look at this pattern, bearing in mind that it's the same whatever size antenna you use. Some of the shot vary in size of course, according to the size of the float, but they go on at the same place.

Let's start from the top. Shot A is unvarying. It's always there in the same position and its sole purpose is to prevent the float from sliding down as far as the bulk shot at B.

The bulk shot vary according to the float. The smallest of the floats shown here will take 2 AAA at point B, the biggest three swans.

These bulk shot are *always* set at four feet from the hook, *regardless of the depth.*

Shot C is our tell-tale for bites and at the same time is useful in preventing tangles. In the diagram we've marked

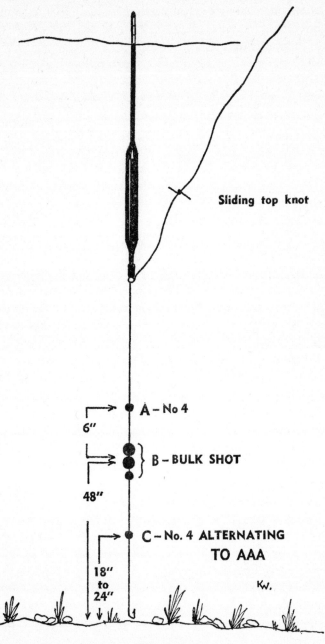

Sliding top knot

A – No 4

6"

B – BULK SHOT

48"

C – No. 4 ALTERNATING
TO AAA

18"
to
24"

K.W.

Fig. 16

it as varying from a No. 4 to an AAA. It's a No. 4 for the smallest float and an AAA for the biggest. The shyer the bite, the nearer the hook it goes.

With the shot placed like this, the terminal tackle travels through the air as straight as it can. But two other things should be borne in mind to make for easier working.

The first is that the bulk shot should be placed on the line so that they touch each other and so that all the slits in each shot are in line. Failure to do this can result in these shots tangling round each other and tying nasty little knots.

The second point is that the cast should always be smooth and underhand. Overhead casts with this gear are risky. You can sometimes get away with it but I never cast this way with slider gear. If you send it flying out underhand, everything will hit the water in its appointed order.

What happens *after* the tackle has reached the baited area is vitally important. With the shots placed as they are the slider float does very definite things which tell you that everything is going according to plan downstairs. It works like this.

When the float hits the water it should lie flat. At this stage leave the pick-up on your casting reel *open*—so that the bulk shot draw line easily through the small float rings.

Immediately the stop-knot reaches the float you will get a positive first setting from the shot at A and B. The moment this happens re-engage the pick-up.

Meanwhile shot C is still on its downward travel. The moment it reaches its full fall, the float will give you a second positive setting, settling lower in the water.

That's the signal to dip your rod tip just under the surface, tightening from the reel to the float and making sure that the line is buried to avoid wind and surface drag. Now you're ready for your first bite!

Generally you will fish the bait just off the bottom if conditions are still. Accurate plumbing at the outset will have achieved this for you. When its rougher you may decide to lay-on.

To lay-on—and bear in mind that with sliding antennas

the water must be still or at the most extremely sluggish—simply move the stop-knot up the line. The first positive setting will be as before but the second and final setting will be delayed, not showing until the last shot, C, has drifted into the laid-on position. It follows that with the tackle set in this way you should be more prepared for lift bites.

Fished off the bottom, the sliding antenna invariably signals bites by going under.

In the laid-on position, the effect of surface drag on the float becomes much greater and when it becomes excessive you may well find that the float won't hold up. The answer is to go in for a light form of float legering.

Fit a Hillman lead—never more than a quarter-ounce and preferably less—on the line above shot C. At the same time move the bulk shot at B a couple of feet *up* the line. The presence of the Hillman will compensate for any casting difficulties.

This variation of the rig does have disadvantages and you may find that even with the Hillman on, the float will still drag under. The answer to this is to take some of the bulk shot at B off the line altogether—the amount being that needed to make sure the float still gives its normal 'show'.

The sliding antenna, then, is a versatile piece of equipment but it does have its limitations. It should never be used in water with even the suggestion of a stream. Still or extremely sluggish waters are the *only* kinds in which it will work properly.

It has the advantage that a bait can be fished just off the bottom at considerable distances in water which is well over the length of the rod. This advantage, to my mind, is at its best in bream waters whereby fishing off bottom you will still interest the bream but dissuade the eels which can be such a nuisance in this setting.

Furthermore it is the perfect wind and drag cheater.

One last point that bears repeating—despite the fact that you are often using a fair amount of shot and a largish float, the fish will still only feel shot C. Any species can be caught on this tackle from the smallest of roach to the biggest of bream.

Understand the tackle and what it is trying to do before you use it and you are half way there. The most important things about learning to use it correctly are mastering the tying of the stop-knot and getting accustomed by instinct to the behaviour of the float as it goes through its different settings. Both rely completely on accurate plumbing at the outset.

A little practice after that and the sliding antenna becomes a new weapon which will bring you more and more fish.

Chapter 6

The sliding porcupine quill

When I first began experimenting with sliding floats—more than ten years ago now—I concentrated my first efforts on a float made of porcupine quill. After a lot of experiments I rejected this material and went on to make my first sliding antenna floats from balsa and cane.

The balsa and cane antenna is a great float and one which is unbeatable on its day. But it has one great limitation in terms of fishing the kind of deep water sliding floats are designed to beat—it's completely useless in running water!

Now there is a lot of good water that is deep AND running. Think of the lower stretches of many of our big tidal rivers. So here was yet another challenge—one which brought me back once more to the idea of the porcupine slider and which resulted in the only float made of this type of quill that I ever use.

One of the sliding antenna's greatest assets—the way in which it allows you to bury the line and beat wind and surface drag—turned out to be the main reason why it was unusable in streamy water. As soon as the current hit that submerged line the float became uncontrollable.

Obviously the way to beat this problem was to invent a trotting float which would be fished from the top, keeping the line on the surface.

In the ordinary way with water within the depth allowed by the rod, the answer would be a fixed Avon, or in a downstream wind a Ducker—buoyant floats which did their job well.

Realising this I felt that buoyancy was going to provide the answer for my problem and what better than a 'porky'— the quill I had always rejected because I felt it to be *too* buoyant?

The sliding antenna had already provided the key clues to fishing sliding gear in deep water—the stop-knot and the small eyelet ring.

I reckoned that by moving the small ring to the tip of the float and by increasing the buoyancy I would have the answer. And so it turned out, with one big difference. The finished float needed two rings instead of one.

The top ring is the small one. Like the ring used for the sliding antenna this is 0.015 in. in diameter. The bottom ring is normal size but when in use it should be pushed back to a slightly offset position to make for more positive locking of the line.

An interesting consequence of the use of two rings and the more positive fixing of the float is that a shot is no longer needed to prevent the float sliding down on to the bulk shot ... a facility which makes for a less complicated method of shotting than that used for the sliding antenna.

It is the use of bulk shot which helped me settle on porcupine quill as the right material for this particular float. With shots spread out, tangles round the tip of a porky are almost inevitable. With bulk shot, the terminal tackle always precedes the quill through the air on the cast, eliminating this common and annoying fault.

This also points to another asset in its favour—the great rigidity of a porky. If you are fishing right across the river you will be giving the float a fair old thump to get it there with a lot of lead on the line. Other quills could easily snap under this treatment—but not the porcupine.

The net result is that here we have a sliding float that will swim a deep stream.

The shotting pattern (see Fig. 17) is very simple and as with the sliding antenna, gives more than one setting ... a

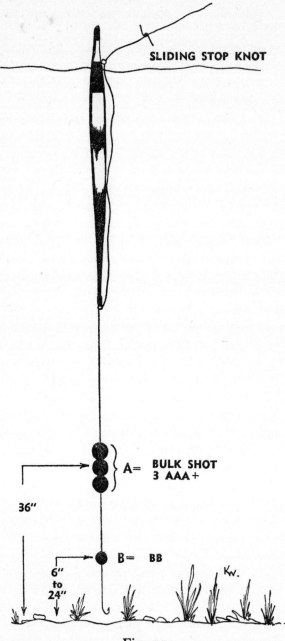

SLIDING STOP KNOT

A= BULK SHOT
3 AAA+

36"

B= BB

6"
to
24"

Kw.

Fig. 17

sequence you must get used to before you can fish the style with confidence.

The first setting comes when the bulk shot—always set three feet from the hook—engage the stop-knot with the top ring. Then comes the pull of your tell-tale shot (B) which gives you your second setting.

The big difference between this and the sliding antenna is that the line is now on the surface. If you watch carefully after the cast you will see a small wake running through the water to the float as the bulk shot do their job ... a good sign that things are working smoothly. Spot that wake— leave the pick-up off to let line run out—and you are well prepared for the first setting of the float, a 'show' of $1\frac{1}{4}$ inches. When the additional weight of shot B pulls down on the knot only half an inch should be left showing.

With these two motions complete you will know all has gone well downstairs.

Because of the extreme buoyancy of porcupine quills—and the thicker they are the better for slider work—the shotting can vary. I've illustrated three AAA for bulk shot but you could need more. If the wind is strong, especially head-on, you might also comfortably increase the weight of shot B, mainly to guard against tangles.

Laying-on with this rig demands care, since you'll be using it in running water, usually with a powerful flow. You need to fish it directly under the rod tip or just downstream of it.

No adjustment is needed for shot B but the bulk shot at A should be moved one or two feet up the line. After that merely move the stop-knot to the required position and be sure to cast slightly out and downstream to ensure proper presentation of the bait.

But it is a dubious gambit and, generally, I much prefer to resort to float-legering when this kind of change is called for with this float. It's advisable, when doing this, to set the rod up at a fairly acute angle to keep as much of the line as possible off the water, reducing the drag which otherwise could pull the tackle under.

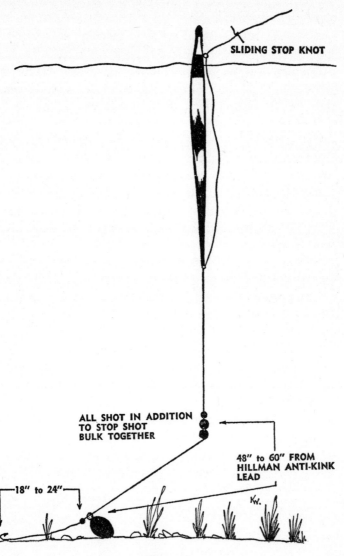

Fig. 18

In other words, you are relying on the weight of the leger pulling against the weight of the float, which in turn is pulling against the rod tip, to give you the necessary amount of show to indicate a bite.

With this set-up (see Fig. 18), you will notice that the bulk shot are fished much farther from the hook ... to compensate first for the depth of water and second for the distance you are fishing. The greater the depth and the longer the cast the farther these shots should be from the hook.

The position of the stop shot for the Hillman lead also varies according to the strength of the flow. The less it is, the nearer you can afford to put this shot to the hook. In my experience, it will be extremely rare for this to be nearer than the maximum setting I have given of 24 inches.

To sum-up, the main point about the sliding porcupine is that it's a float for deep running water. You could fish it in still water but it would be nothing like so effective as the sliding antenna—mainly because you are losing that valuable facility of being able to bury the line.

One other rather foxy point about this float is that where you are fishing in an extremely wide water, you may find it necessary when float legering to fish well over depth to get a correct setting of the float for bite indication. In these circumstances, if the water was 14 ft. deep you may find it necessary to set the float at 20 ft., at the same time altering your shot accordingly.

The sliding porcupine quill is an extremely useful float, bridging a gap in deep water fishing that the antenna cannot cover.

It's been a match winner for me several times.

Chapter 7

Top ring sliders and the Missile

For ninety-nine per cent of my angling time when conditions dictate the use of a sliding float, the cane and balsa antenna or the sliding porcupine quill are adequate for my needs.

But not always. And the odd occasions when they aren't are the few when I resort to the floats discussed in this Chapter.

They are, in fact, substitutes for the better known sliding 'porky' and sliding antenna floats dealt with in the last two chapters. They work in the same category of water—deep running swims and deep still water. But only in certain special conditions.

I certainly use them less than any others in my tackle box. But having pledged myself to be complete on the subject of float fishing I feel bound to include them.

It goes without saying that the times when I do use them are occasions when they're the *only* ones which will do the job.

The first of them, float A, is the one which can replace the sliding porcupine quill in extremely turbulent running water. The second, float B, is a change float for the sliding antenna in unusual stillwater conditions.

Let's deal with them in that order.

Now where you get a deep running water swim that is extremely turbulent or boily, together with an excessively strong and deep undercurrent, the sliding porcupine, good as it is, has a job holding up in a way that makes it certain you will spot bites.

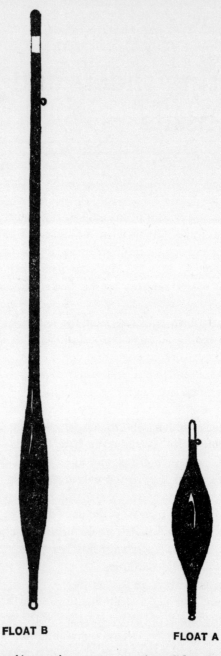

FLOAT B

FLOAT A

Right (Float A) running water top ring slider. Left (Float B) still water top ring slider. The upper rings are 15/1000ths of an inch in diameter.

Water of this power is uncommon in England but where you do find it, this substitute float is just the ticket. A typical example would be the Lower Severn in that rough old section between Upton and Tewkesbury. Even if I was trotting fairly close to the bank here, I'd use this bulbous-looking float.

As you can see from looking at it, the float has some of the assets of the antenna plus two float rings, one at top and bottom.

The bulbous body of the float—you can see it's fatter than an antenna—is designed to hold the tip to the surface in a way that will keep it clear through the boils. This process is considerably helped by having the small ring—not less than 0.015 in. in diameter as before—at the top.

This so-sensitive tip is particularly useful when, during the swim, the float crosses the crease between extremely fast and slacker water.

A look at the diagram (Fig. 19) shows that the float is fixed to the line like the sliding porcupine quill.

The bulk shot shown here is comparatively light at three AAA plus. That's the lightest I would go which means that you need more than one size of this float going up to one big enough to carry as many as four swans.

This bulk shot is *always* fixed at the same distance from the hook—three feet. Shot B is the normal tell-tale for bites, its distance from the hook being governed by the usual reason, the strength of the bites.

In water like the Lower Severn you will find that you can get tremendous depth variations in one swim. At one point it will be 18 ft., at another 14 ft. while at a third, it's 16 ft.

With a rig like this you'll find the bait lifts easily, taking these variations in its stride. It will do it in a way which means you do not severely have to mend line, causing those jerks in mid-trot which, as I've mentioned before, can be so alarming to the fish.

You should never use this float in still water nor should you ever attempt to lay-on with it. It offers so much resistance to the current, all you'd get would be a constant series

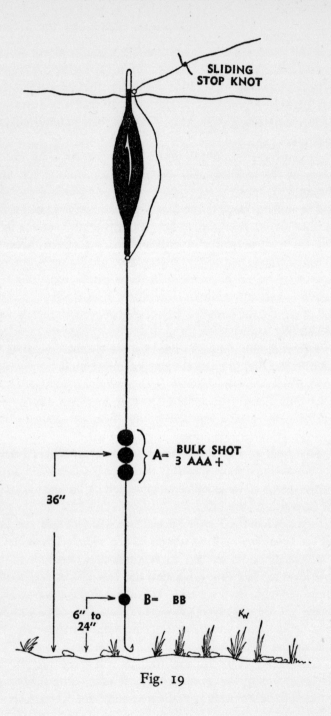

Fig. 19

of false bites. For the same reason it follows that I would never float-leger with it.

When this chap failed it would be a case of straight legering.

And now the second float (float B), the still-water substitute for a sliding antenna. As you can see it has a much longer antenna than the other, with the small top ring whipped on about one inch from the tip.

A typical still or slightly sluggish water where I'd use this float would be the Middle Level Drain in Cambridgeshire, a water which is not only deep close to the bank but one where I'm also likely to catch fish at close quarters, too.

I'd be fishing not more than one rod length out from the bank with this float and my basic reason for favouring it over the normal sliding antenna is that in such a situation you can get away with much less shot.

Fishing the centre of the Middle Level I'd maybe use a normal one-ring sliding antenna carrying as much as three swan shot. With this close-quarters variation I can get the same efficiency with the equivalent of only one swan—and indeed I'd never go heavier than that.

If, on the other hand, I cast this variation way out, I'd find the float cocking *before* the bulk shot had pulled line through the top ring to the stop-knot ... giving a false impression that the float was fishing correctly.

By fishing close at hand and having that top ring, I can lift the rod up in the air to speed the pull of the line through the top ring, getting rid of resistance from the rod tip and surface drag.

If you know the water I am talking about and others like it, it should also have followed that I'm looking for roach for makeweight with this float, after deciding that there are no far out bream wanting to have a go.

In other words, close-range, deep, light fishing—the sort you can't afford to try with the normal sliding antenna.

The shotting pattern for this change float is the same as for its running-water companion except that the bulk shot is much lighter ... say one AAA and one BB.

Now there's one more slider I want to discuss, but before I do let's re-cap on those I've covered so far.

The one-ring sliding antenna (the ring is tiny and at the bottom) should only be used in still water where long casting is required and where the water is never less than eight feet deep.

The two-ring sliding porcupine (the small ring is at the top) should only be used in running water where, once again, the depth is not less than eight feet and where the swim is not over turbulent or blessed with strong undercurrents.

The first of the two-ring specials should only be used in the most turbulent running water while the second should only be used in still water when fishing close to the bank.

And don't forget that stop-knot. It could make or break all your efforts. It should be tight enough on the line so that it is virtually impossible to move when the line slackens. And the ends should have been trimmed to not less than one inch so that it slips easily through the rod rings on the cast.

And the other slider I want to mention? It's my latest invention and came into existence as a result of Coventry's plans to fish the 1967 National Championship in the Relief Channel.

For those who have never been there, it's a big, wide, deep water ... the only kind, in fact, where this particular float and the long, long casting it permits comes into its own.

We soon found that the new float not only flew through the air with the greatest of ease. It did it mighty accurately, too. During tests, there was naturally a lot of talk about it and one of the chance remarks made at this time led to the float finally being christened.

The remark? 'It goes through the air just like a guided missile!' The general feeling was that to refer to it constantly as the 'guided missile' was a bit too clumsy so we ended up calling it simply ... THE MISSILE.

At least, it's got a nice 20th century sound to it!

Now as many of you will know, the missile brought me no luck at all in that ill-fated Championship match. I was one of the hundreds waterlicked on a day which produced the worst ever return for our highly rated Coventry team. But at least I can say now that I came out of that match with a new float which has since proved to be one of the most useful I've ever invented in terms of the specific job it was expected to do.

To help you get the picture more, let's refer back to the Relief Channel. Faced with such a water, most anglers, I suppose, would resort to the leger with a swing tip or bite indicator especially as even the biggest existing floats of the sliding variety just didn't have the flying power to take the tackle the extreme distances required.

But we felt a float was still the answer—if one could be found. This was the general opinion of our team after it became obvious during discussions that several members of the side had been extremely successful on this water with a float with the bait fished on a long, slow drop with light terminal tackle because fish were often located well off the bottom.

Alternatively, by nailing the bait to the bottom with a leger lead we were running the serious risk of putting the bait BELOW the fish and giving ourselves time wasting trouble changing tackle if you wanted to look higher in the water.

The answer then was a float which would carry light terminal tackle as far as we wanted and which could be easily adjusted to fish at various depths. This, we reasoned, would give us the same advantage as the leger men with the added facility of being able to move about the various levels in the water much more easily.

Dare I add, too, that such a float would also bring the indication of the bite much nearer the fish than it would with a tip—a point my opponents of the leger know I feel pretty strongly about and one I have yet to feel calls for any change on my part.

No one is going to tell me that a swing tip angler in a water like the Channel is going to get earlier notice of a bite than an angler fishing with a float directly over the bait

... especially at the kind of distances I'm going to be talking about now.

I have also heard it said—and recently, too—that the man who uses a swing tip gets half an hour more fishing time in a five hour match because of the speed with which he can put his bait where he wants it in the water. To me, this is just another red herring and a suggestion I reject completely. For it's my opinion that a good float angler can not only match the 'tipper' for speed, he can beat him! Let's face it, you have only to watch some leger anglers after they have cast and they are taking painstaking seconds—sometimes even minutes—to make sure everything is tight to that lead. The float angler does not have this problem—especially with a weapon like the missile. He merely casts it out to where he wants it and all the time that bait is falling he is in line for a bite.

The missile, in fact, solves all the problems I've just mentioned. Its great and most obvious advantage is the ease with which it permits you to cast long distances with little effort —and by long distances I am talking of *at least 50 yards*!

It follows that the missile can be fished literally as far as you are capable of throwing your groundbait because, believe me, the float will always go further if you want it to.

The dodge is to cast the float *beyond* the baited area winding it back quickly to the bait and thus burying the line *deeply* under the surface to prevent wind and surface drag on the line. When you understand this message, you will realise immediately why the missile is 16 in. long.

In other words, it's got all the advantages of the biggest sliding antenna multiplied twice over.

Having, I suppose, bragged a little about the great casting advantage of the missile, let me immediately admit that I can't throw groundbait 50 yards but nor, I'd guess, could most leger anglers. But until the missile came along, the leger man did have a casting advantage. Now he's lost it.

At extreme distance, mind you, I reckon I have another advantage. Once the leger man's bomb has gone under the surface he's got a heck of a job on placing his bait accurately in the chosen area. Being able to get a float like the missile the same distance means that I have a built-in marker buoy in the shape of the float for baiting. To hold his own in these circumstances, the leger man has to cast with 100 per cent accuracy *every time* and do likewise with his bait ... and that, in terms of the distances we are talking about, is something few can do.

It boils down to this. If you are strong enough to throw your bait 60 yards you could fish accurately over it with the missile with no trouble at all.

Judging from the gasps I got from my gallery on the Channel, I decided that half of it was surprise at how far I really did throw the bait and the rest at how easily I made sure float tackle followed it to just the right spot.

But the Channel is not the only water where the missile can be useful. The lower Great Ouse and the Nene are two more. It would also be fine for distance fishing in lakes and reservoirs where the water was deep. It will fish still or sluggish water but is *useless* in flowing water with any strength to speak of to the current.

In match terms, it's been used with most success so far on the North Bank of the Nene. Two Coventry anglers won matches with the missile *before* the Relief Channel National and I was second in another event also using the float. With these results to go on, I'm sure you'll all see why we had so much faith in it for the Channel.

Once I knew the problems that had to be solved with the missile float, the shape of the thing became immediately obvious. Not so easy was the choice of materials.

But eventually I solved it—and by using one material in particular which I'd always previously rejected for float making.

I'm talking about the long piece of peacock quill which forms the stem of the float.

While I know many anglers, especially my friends in the North, have long favoured this quill for floats I have always steered clear of it for I felt that, as a natural quill, it was far too buoyant.

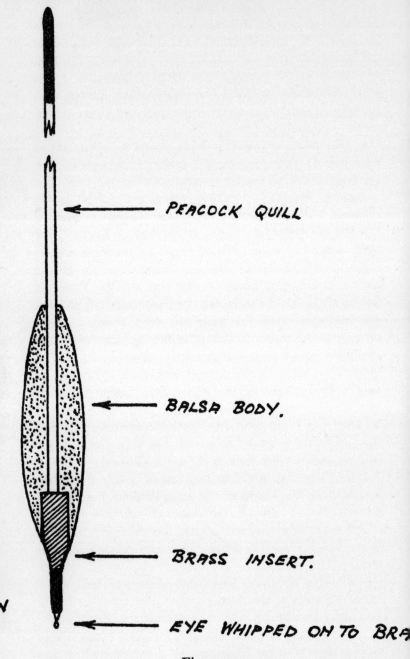

PEACOCK QUILL

BALSA BODY.

BRASS INSERT.

EYE WHIPPED ON TO BRA[SS]

Kw

Fig. 20

Billy displays a fine roach catch taken from the River Tweed at Norham trotting with an Avon float.

Take cover is a basic angling tenet and Billy always makes the most of any he can find. In this picture he is playing a lively Wind-rush chub taken trotting with his Trout Trotter float.

Used, however, as it is with the missile, it's just the job, working, as it does, in competition with a balsa body loaded with a brass rod at the base. The balance achieved in the little tug of war between the materials used in the float makes it just perfect.

The quill varies in length so that the finished float in its various sizes is no less than 16 in. and no more than 18 in. The balsa body, in all cases, is three inches long and, as you can see from the diagram (Fig. 20), the peacock stem sits on top of the brass loading inside this body.

The float ring, which is whipped on to the brass where it protrudes from the lower end of the balsa body, is the small-eyed type as used for the sliding antenna. Its diameter is 0.015 in.

The three sizes of this float I carry are based on a shot loading equivalent to a total of one swan, two swan and three swan. As you will discover I don't use exactly these shots but the total weight of those I do tallies with them.

The shotting pattern (Fig. 21) is similar to that used for the sliding antenna and, like the latter, this float works against a sliding knot.

But mark these shotting details carefully or you could run into trouble.

Now if the wind is blowing from behind you, everything should be plain sailing. But if it's coming from any other direction, problems are likely with this float.

You see the missile travels—as its name suggests—extremely fast, so fast that it tends to precede the shots through the air therefore leaving you prone to back tangles. You get round this by increasing the size of the last shot on the line (shot C). With the missile, this should never ever be smaller than a BB and more often than not it will be a AAA or, on some occasions, even as big as a swan.

Don't let this worry you in terms of offering extra resistance to the fish because the rig is so well balanced this simply doesn't happen and don't forget to compensate for any change with the bulk shot to retain balance.

As on previous occasions, this tell-tale shot (C) is an

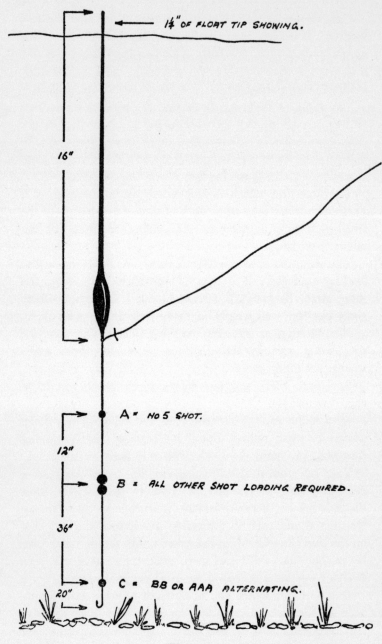

Fig. 21

alternator and should be moved nearer the hook if bites are shy but never, with this float, any nearer than 20 inches for remember the shallowest water you'd fish with the missile is 14 ft.

Next up the line are the bulk shot. Generally they want to be three feet above the tell-tale shot but in really deep water I'd stick them another six inches further up the line. Shot A (12 in. above the bulk) is there to prevent the float sliding down on to the bulk shot. Above the float, of course, is your sliding knot. This knot is also the thing which enables you to vary the depth at which you are fishing so easily merely by moving it up or down the line.

It is, by the way, perfectly all right to lay-on with the missile, i.e. with shot C sitting on the bed of the river.

As for plumbing the depth, it is best with the missile, as with all the other sliders, to do this with the required shot already fixed on the line.

And now the question I've most often been asked by those anglers who have seen me using the missile—why is it so big? The idea of its extra length is to really get the line buried under the surface away from drag of all kinds.

The cast with this tackle is underhand. This is always best with bottom ring floats of the sliding variety for it ensures that everything enters the water in the right order. In this case, of course, the cast is to a point *beyond* the baited area to permit the tackle to be drawn back over the bait.

Once this has been done—and only then—dip the rod tip under the surface then open the pick-up on your casting reel so that the shots can draw line freely through the float ring. This action will, at the same time, sink the line for you.

The first positive indication that all is going well comes when the knot reaches the float ring—and in the case of the missile different things happen according to the size of the float you are using.

With the smaller version (i.e. the 16 in. float) you get a sure indication immediately the knot reaches the float. The float sits in the water with about eight inches of the stem showing. As the rest of the shots descend, two more settings follow, the first when the bulk shot find their position and the last when the tell-tale is in place. You'll get used to the sequence of these events and how long they take. If any of them fail to happen or one of them is running late—strike!

With the larger floats the pattern of behaviour is slightly different. The two-swan shot versions will leave about 12 in. showing on the first setting before going through the other movements and the three-swan version will at first lie flat like the sliding antenna only giving you a first setting when the bulk shot pull the knot to the float ring.

I mention these in detail for without knowing this you might think the floats should all work the same and that something was up.

After the final setting, re-engage the pick-up and gently tighten to the float.

There is, of course, good reason for having missiles which take differing amounts of lead. In really deep water—and I'm thinking of 20 ft. plus—it's better to add more weight downstairs on the line than to the brass loading in the float. It will give you a more positive setting and, in addition, reduces the time you have to wait for everything to settle down.

On the other hand, if the water is not too deep, the one-swan version is quite adequate to achieve the necessary.

To some extent, I suppose, the missile is a limited float. It's only of use to you when you want to fish at extreme distances in extremely deep water. But then no other float is capable of doing this job. For that reason I'd urge you all to master the missile technique and get yourself equipped with one.

Which reminds me that I ought to warn you that they are a nuisance to carry for few float boxes or, indeed, baskets can accommodate a float 16 in. long, especially when it's got to be protected against breakage. You could make your float so that the quill stem is detachable or—and this is what we've done—make a pocket for it somewhere on your holdall.

Chapter 8

The zoomer

When these floats were first introduced, they got a great deal of publicity. Too much, in my opinion, for it's now obvious their importance was not as great as the headlines suggested. They are, in fact, useful additions to any tackle box but, as I hope to demonstrate, much more limited in their uses than many imagine.

It was in the lower River Welland in Lincolnshire where the zoomer first came into its own and indeed this water is the perfect definition of the type which calls for the use of these floats.

It's not deep—about seven feet at most. But there is generally a need to cast a bait a long distance while retaining the utmost sensitivity in the tackle below the float.

To the best of my knowledge, the zoomer was conceived by anglers from Leicester and it was they who made the impact with it in the Welland which led to those headlines I mentioned earlier.

To me, at the time it seemed a logical development from the big cork and quill duckers with which our Coventry team had then so recently scored in the 1956 Witham National. Whether this was how it looked to the Leicester lads I don't know.

But what is certain is that the zoomer had all, and perhaps more, of the long-distance casting advantages of the big ducker without the need to carry so much lead below the float.

This was achieved by moulding lead carefully into the body of the zoomer in a way which ensured that its streamlined shape was retained and giving it the action of a dart on the cast.

The stem at the bottom of the float is made of brass giving support to the lead at the lower end of the body and carrying the float ring. It also plays an important part in giving added weight to this end of the float. The upper stem, or antenna, is of cane and it joins the lower brass stem inside the float body which is made of balsa wood.

The length of the brass piece varies according to the amount of lead you want the float to carry and that, in its turn, varies according to the size of the float.

Making zoomers is a long and tedious job and wherever you find yourself able to buy the right quality article I advise you to do this every time.

Should you find yourself forced to begin making these floats yourself, let me give you a little tip. As long as you obtain a reasonable line to the body you'll be all right. And —another useful tip—the easiest way to get lead to fit the float is to buy a selection of barrel leads from your local tackle shop and cut them according to the size of zoomer you want to make.

Furthermore, while it's best to have the lower stem made of brass, it doesn't have to be this material. You'll get away with using cane though this will not make for such a satisfactory downward weighting of the float. But it will still work.

In many ways, of course, these zoomers look much like the sliding antennas I recently dealt with at length. But don't let this fool you—the functions of the two floats are entirely different.

The sliding antenna, I hope you will recall, is for long-distance fishing in still, deep water with the weight downstairs on the line to carry the bait reasonably quickly to the fish and pull the line through the bottom ring.

The zoomer is designed for fishing shallow water at long distances with the further advantage that the float is fixed and carries less weight. It has one other scoring point over the sliding antenna, which is very much a still-water float.

The zoomer can be used in still-water AND in water which has a steady—and I mean really steady—flow.

At this stage I'd better say that the zoomer can be used on the slide. While many do use it in this way it is not, in my opinion, satisfactory for fishing the deeper sort of water which would have led you to require a sliding float.

There are several reasons for this. When you are casting long distances you get a lot of line drag and resistance from the water itself. You are fishing with less shot on the line than you would with an antenna and the zoomer, because it is semi self-cocking, tends to cock too soon. The net result means that the line is not pulled through the tiny float ring needed for slider fishing as easily as it ought to be.

The disastrous consequence of this—and one which for me makes the zoomer an abortion for slider fishing—is that the float will *look* as though it is fishing correctly when in fact your bait is not where you want it to be at all.

In other words, if you were fishing 12 ft. of water and wanted the bait just off the bottom, the zoomer could still look all right if the bait had actually stopped falling at a depth of only 6 ft. or 7 ft. Your stop-knot wouldn't be anywhere near the bottom ring yet—but you wouldn't have any good way of knowing that.

But that's not the end of it. Once the float has settled in this halfway position, worse begins to happen. Every so often a little bit more line will tend to pass through the small eye. When this happens you think you are getting a lift bite. But of course, there's nothing there.

It can be a pretty nerve-wracking business as I once discovered when a friend of mine fished a zoomer on the slide for a whole morning. He was absolutely bamboozled by lunchtime. 'Do you know,' he said, 'I've been getting fabulous bites for three hours and I haven't hit a single fish.'

When I told him the answer and he switched to the normal sliding antenna he went on to have a pleasant afternoon with the added bonus of a lesson about sliding zoomers well learned. The zoomer fished as a slider has another nasty trait in my experience. It tends to move about all over the place, mostly because of that surface drag.

Having got that little piece of prejudice off my chest, let me sum up with a few basic thoughts about zoomers before going on, to tell you about how to fish it. See it solely as a fixed float. Realise in doing so that you will only use it at limited depths—say not more than 8 ft. and not less than 3 ft.

Understand its basic purpose—to enable you to fish reasonably light at long distances whatever the strength or direction of the wind.

And the best key to understanding the zoomer is, as I mentioned earlier, the river which inspired its invention, the Welland. Now the Welland, in the lower reaches where the float is used, is fairly wide and sluggish and to catch bream one has to fish right across the river under the far bank.

For this job a sliding antenna—with the amount of weight it can carry—would do.

But by using it in this way one would be making it do something for which it was not designed.

The trick, then, was to find a float which was fixed, but which would have the distance casting advantages of the antenna. The answer was the zoomer.

Having found this solution, zoomer anglers soon went on to discover that the lighter shotting downstairs, permitted by the float's lead loading, also gave them a greater freedom of shotting. In the diagram (Fig. 22), you will see the shotting pattern which is virtually basic for zoomer fishing.

Look first at the shot between rod and float. This shot is there because, when float-fishing at long distances, I think it vital to well and truly bury under the surface the line between rod and float—thus gaining maximum protection from wind and surface drag.

Note this is an alternating shot in terms of size and distance. The stronger the drag, the bigger the shot should be. The deeper the water, and the greater the distance you are fishing, the farther this shot should be from the float. Distance and shot sizes, though, should be kept within those illustrated in the diagram.

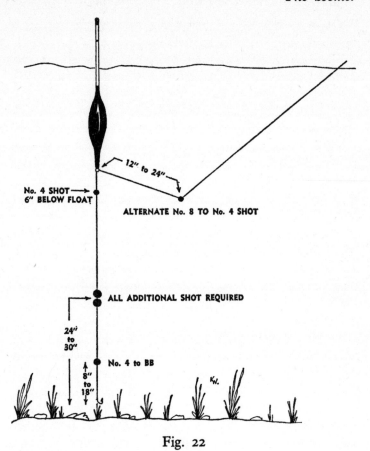

No. 4 SHOT →
6" BELOW FLOAT

12" to 24"

ALTERNATE No. 8 TO No. 4 SHOT

ALL ADDITIONAL SHOT REQUIRED

24"
to
30"

No. 4 to BB

8"
to
18"

Fig. 22

Consider next the number four shot, six inches below the float. This is a tell-tale for depth. A glance at it will tell you immediately if your float has slipped on the line, and— if you have made changes during the day—it will also indicate your starting depth after the initial plumbing.

As with the sliding antenna the bulk shot can be seen lumped together to avoid back tangles on the cast. I have no hard-and-fast rules on the size of these shots because if you go in for zoomer fishing properly you will have a number of different-sized floats.

The bulk shot can, therefore, vary a great deal. Indeed, with zoomers now being used in waters ranging from small canals to rivers like the Welland, the bulk shot can vary from as little as one No. 6 up to two swans.

The distance at which these bulk shots are placed from the hook is settled by the same criterion used for the sliding antenna: the depth of the water.

In other words, the deeper the water the farther the bulk shots are placed from the hook. Incidentally, I hope by now that it's unnecessary to add that the lower shot is the bite tell-tale which moves nearer the hook as the fish get shyer.

Like a number of floats already dealt with in this series, the zoomer has shotting which could be described as different from the normal.

This changed shotting can cause a lot of trouble for those who will insist that their cast be overhand.

The reason is simple. There is a more positive snatch given to the tackle by an overhand throw—and this is particularly true when the float is of the loaded variety like the zoomer.

An underhand cast is much the best for getting your tackle out as this allows everything to wing its way across the water in the correct order. More important, it also ensures that everything hits the surface in the right sequence.

But for those died-in-the-wool overhanders who find it difficult to accept my advice, there is a way with the zoomer which will allow them to stick to their old ways.

This is achieved by sliding the majority of the bulk shot farther up the line towards the float.

If you do this, you must make sure there's still sufficient weight left lower down the line to prevent this part of the tackle holding back. In most cases the re-arranged pattern will consist of the bulk shot placed 6 in. from the float— or even directly beneath it—and one reasonably heavy shot —a AAA or a swan—20 in. from the hook.

But if you still get tangles with this, or any other arrangement, you will know that you haven't left sufficient weight downstairs and you will have to experiment further.

Incidentally, I would mention here that the changed system which I have just outlined is the way to set your tackle—even for underhand casting—if the wind is head-on. This is a general instruction for all floats of the antenna type when in a facing wind you should vary your shotting in exactly the same way with a sliding antenna.

Now zoomers used for rivers like the Welland, the Cam and similar wide waters, are medium to large in size. But for canal work, a much smaller float of the same design should be used. In this context it's best to think of this mini-zoomer as an alternative to the Dart which I described earlier in this book.

The size of a zoomer used for canal work should be 5 in. long at the most, with a slim body, and 4 in. at the least. Its shotting capacity will be between four No. 4 and two No. 6.

The shotting pattern is similar to that for the reverse crowquill except that when four No. 4 are used, three should be placed directly under the float and the fourth, 20 inches from the hook. When using a float which calls for the equivalent of two No. 6, I put a No. 8 dust shot alternating near the hook, a No. 6 twenty inches from the hook, and a further No. 8 between the float and rod-tip to sink the line.

The only change to this pattern is when the bait used is caster. Because caster itself has some real weight, my first shot above the hook would be a dust at 20 in. while all the bulk would be directly under the float. The shot used for sinking the line between rod and float, incidentally, should never be bigger than a dust when fishing a canal.

And so, in the way I have described, the zoomer has achieved the same purpose on a canal as it does on a bigger river—distance coupled with lightness.

In saying this, I realise that many stick float fans will prick up their ears. Stick floats have become something of a vogue in canals, but not for me. I would always rather use a crowquill where possible—and where not, a mini-zoomer or dart.

I would add that stick floats are remarkably good in certain circumstances and I will be dealing with them shortly.

Meanwhile, don't get carried away by zoomers. They are definitely not a versatile float and certainly nothing like as useful as some people insist. Their use should be restricted to those occasions where long casting is required in reasonably shallow and still waters, *and no others.*

If you bear this in mind—and don't attempt tactics like laying-on—you will find them the useful, occasional float they really are.

Chapter 9

The stick float

There has probably never been a float which has made such an impact on the angling world as the ubiquitous stick— that slim float from Lancashire with which more people seem to have won more matches and caught more fish in recent years than with any other.

Yet the truth, in my opinion, about this much publicised float is something else, so much so that, while I am including it here, I must insist at the outset that all those stories about it have given the float a false reputation. The stick in fact, is not a miracle worker. Indeed, it is one of the most limited floats imaginable.

When I first wrote about them even I was to a certain extent hooked on sticks and at that time I said that, given the right conditions in the right water on the right day, the stick was absolutely unbeatable.

Now I don't think that any more and, in fact, I now reject completely the conventional cane and balsa stick float in all my fishing though, as you will discover, I have come to have an ever-increasing regard for the other form of stick, the wire-stemmed stick.

But I am racing ahead. This is a controversial float and I think that to understand it best it's important to get it properly in perspective.

Now in a lot of these matches we heard so much about when the stick first came to the fore, I think it must be borne in mind that by that time practically everyone was using one and therefore a winner more often than not turned out to be a stick float angler. But, given different float tackle in many of these same matches, the same man would still have won and probably with a lot more fish.

Now the stick revolution undoubtedly began in Lancashire and its development was, I would say, entirely due to the emergence of casters as bait. In fact, had it not been for the link between these two things I feel quite certain that far less would have been heard about the stick than has been.

All this brings me to my first and most important point. The stick is, in many respects, a one bait float and that bait is, of course, caster.

Because of all that publicity I have mentioned far too many anglers have come to the conclusion that it's virtually *the* passport to success when it is merely one more kind of float which, at certain times, can have its uses.

It's best now, perhaps, to look at the sort of waters where sticks are at their best and these are streamy, but not turbulent, rivers where the depth is not great, the Trent being a perfect example. In other words, it's a float for trotting water where the trotting is not too difficult.

On the other hand, many Lancashire anglers swear by the stick in canals but I am utterly opposed to this favouring myself small zoomers or that other new float so recently introduced, the Dart.

But it isn't just the water that has to be right for the stick. Wind conditions must be simply perfect or its use is a complete waste of time. You need an upstream wind or one blowing from behind and you should never try to fish a stick with the wind in your face or when it's blowing downstream.

In many ways the conventional sticks—those made with a cane stem and a balsa tip—are similar to the simple crowquill and they are only preferred because that form of construction I have just mentioned makes the float more buoyant at the tip giving it its main advantage, better control between rod tip and float. Its heavier weight also offers a casting advantage while retaining sensitivity.

Properly made the stick is a semi self-cocking float. Because the lower part of it, the cane, is heavier than the

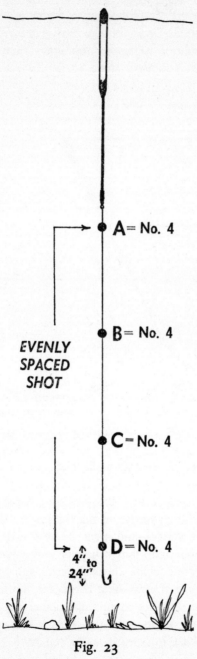

A = No. 4

B = No. 4

*EVENLY
SPACED
SHOT*

C = No. 4

D = No. 4

4" to
24""

Fig. 23

tip, an unshotted stick would sit in the water at an angle and not lie flat. A lot of anglers who have corresponded with me have had trouble in achieving this inner balance within the float and it is a difficult thing to do. Indeed, it's just one more reason why I've come to reject the conventionally made sticks for my own fishing.

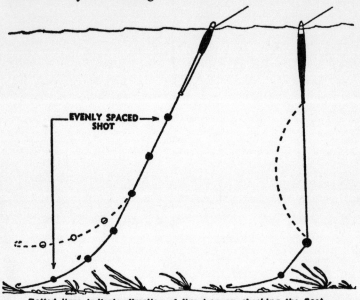

EVENLY SPACED SHOT

Dotted lines indicate direction of line-drag on checking the float.

Fig. 24

The method of shotting stick floats is invariably the same (Fig. 23), that is with leads of an even size pinched on equidistant from each other, the last shot being an alternator depending on the strength of the bites.

The object of this—and it can be used with other floats— is to make the right things happen downstairs particularly when the tackle is being checked on its way down the swim.

The best way of explaining this is for you to imagine first that we have *not* shotted in this manner but have put our bulk shot about 18 in. from the hook. When you hold tackle set like this back in streamy water you get a bow in the line underwater in a downstream direction (see Fig 24). It

Dusk is falling and the fight is over as Billy prepares to net a Lochmaben bream ... taken this time on a swing-tip.

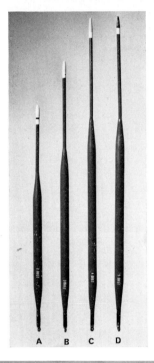

Billy Lane's complete set of dart floats. The dimensions and shot carry capacities for these floats are as follows: float A stem overall length 5 in., body 3 in., body width (standard on all lengths) $\frac{1}{4}$ in., shotting 2 dust; float B stem 6 in., body $2\frac{1}{2}$ in., shotting 3 dust; floats C and D stem 7 in., body $4\frac{1}{2}$ in., shotting 4 or 5 dust, the difference being achieved by varying the loading of the body in the float (see Chapter 2).

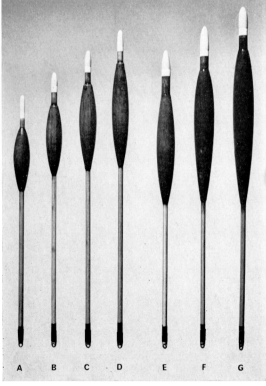

This picture shows a complete set of Billy Lane's Avon floats and for do-it-yourself float makers this is the check list on dimensions and shot carrying capacities: float A stem $5\frac{1}{2}$ in., body $1\frac{1}{4}$ in. (3BB); float B stem 6 in., body $1\frac{1}{2}$ in. (4BB) float C stem $6\frac{1}{2}$ in., body $1\frac{7}{8}$ in. (5BB); float D stem 7 in., body $2\frac{1}{2}$ in. (6BB), float E $6\frac{1}{2}$ in., body $2\frac{1}{2}$ in. (2 swan); float F stem 7 in., body 3 in. ($2\frac{1}{2}$ swan); float G stem $7\frac{1}{2}$ in., body $3\frac{1}{2}$ in. (3 swan) (see Chapter 3).

follows that if a fish chose to take at this moment it would have to pull the bow out of the line before any indication of its action was shown on the float and this is, in fact, the main reason why tackle set like this to interest fish feeding deep should never be held back in this way.

By setting the leads evenly that bow is prevented when the tackle is checked. In this setting the tackle, on checking, merely leads to a natural lifting of the line between float and hook in a downstream direction so that the taking fish still immediately gives a signal on the float.

Now this even method of shotting is, like the float itself, closely tied up with that link between stick floats and casters. I am, of course, referring to the way in which caster anglers feed their swims. They don't groundbait heavily and on most occasions use none at all.

In waters like the Trent—a typical stick water—they normally feed two pints of casters or more during a match or pleasure stint and they put them in loose so that the fish are taking them at constantly varying depths.

From this it will be clear that the caster angler with his stick float shotted in the way I have illustrated can attract fish at these varying levels merely by checking the float. In fact, one of the deadliest ways of fishing casters is to use them with the float held back in fits and jerks on its way down through the swim.

The tackle itself is invariably set deeper than the depth at which you are fishing to better facilitate this searching action I have mentioned. If, for example, the swim averaged four feet in depth, you would set the float five feet above the hook.

When you cast you should give the tackle an immediate check which will produce a tight line to your float and make certain that the bait is moving off down the swim ahead of the float and *off* the bottom. When it's released you have a perfect two-way tension between rod and float and shots to float.

Because the stick is so easy to control this balance created by the line tight to the float gives you a natural hold on the

H

tackle which would be extremely tricky, if not impossible, to achieve with many other running water floats such as the Avons. At the same time it is because this balance is so fine that conditions must be absolutely right for stick float fishing and therein, of course, lie its limitations. By checking the float at intervals down the swim you can search the water all the time and, I would emphasise, fish will most often take at these moments of checking and you should always be ready at these times.

I cannot advise you to read this last passage too carefully for it gives the key to the relationship between the stick float and caster fishing. The hovering effect which the checking of the float gives the bait, thanks, as I hope I have demonstrated, to the shotting, is the main reason why this is such a successful rig.

Another reason why evenly spaced shots are such an advantage with casters is that, in my opinion, fish like to take a caster slowly. They like to consider it and, perhaps, mouth it before making the final, fatal chew. This shotting system permits them to do this with no risk of the shots pulling the bait out of the fish's mouth.

Basically, we fish casters with the stick over-depth to get the best results and, normally, would always begin by fishing in this way. But there is one exception to this and that is where the water is heated by outfalls from such bankside installations as power stations, a thing which occurs often in rivers like the Trent and the Calder.

In this setting fish rarely hang about near the bottom. They are swimming at all depths because of the extreme fermentation and souring which takes place on the bed of rivers in sections like this. And that is why in such places I would think nothing of fishing anything between 1 ft. and 3 ft. *under* depth. I would still retain that so-important checking ability but would be saving time because I am no longer searching a part of the river which contained nothing.

Some anglers also use stick floats for still water conditions in which instance they merely fix the float at the lower end instead of top and bottom, a system which is known in some parts of the country as 'pegging'.

I don't like this method myself for I think that the strike is seriously impaired and that, in any case, there are other floats far, far superior for this job, for example the simple crowquill, the reverse crowquill, the onion, the dart, the duckers and the sliders.

I would like now to refer again to my earlier statement to the effect that I have rejected the conventional stick in favour of the more recently introduced wire stemmed version version of this float.

To me it has, at once, converted it from a very limited angling weapon into one which is much more versatile. If you remember I said earlier that stick floats were not effective in swims which were at all boily or turbulent. Such things are no problem to the wire stick which, however, has another even greater advantage which is that it is much simpler to make than the cane and balsa model.

All it is is a slim piece of balsa with a stiff wire stem, piano wire being one of the best materials to use for the latter because it is so rigid. This has, of course, led to a basic change in the nature of the float. In the conventional stick the buoyancy is created by the tug of war between the cane and balsa sections of the float.

With the wire stick *all* the buoyancy has been centred in the tip which explains why it can cope with rougher waters than the earlier model.

The advantage of all this is that anglers faced with fairly turbulent water need no longer resort to the Avons and the heavier shotting they require, shotting which could prove too heavy for the smaller stamp of fish encountered in waters like the Trent. With the wire stick light shotting, to exactly the same pattern as before, is possible. Nowadays I have wire sticks in my basket which carry up to 8 BB shot and I find them a great asset as they form a useful alternative to try before committing yourself to the use of the heavier Avon.

Shotting with sticks has generally to be extremely exact and most anglers I know have a code of markings for their collection of stick floats which enables them to shot them up correctly at a glance. This is a system I would urge anyone to copy.

Now one last point before I sum up about these floats. Laying-on, in the true sense of the phrase, is not really possible with the stick. By this I mean that you lay-on—but with a difference. The even spaced shotting pattern remains the same and the float is set to fish 50 per cent over depth but when the tackle is in the water you don't, as you normally would, let it lie still for long periods. You cast, let it pause, and then allow the bait to move downstream; another pause, and then repeat the operation.

To sum up about sticks, don't use them when the wind is downstream or in your face. Don't use them in still waters. Don't use the conventional cane and balsa stick in turbulent swims. Never be afraid to check the tackle during trotting. Always fish a reasonable limit over depth and always maintain a tight line between rod tip and float when doing so.

Chapter 10

The Trent Trotter

Many of the great breakthroughs in angling techniques have been made by chance. And none came more by chance than the float I want to tell you about now ... a float which gave me a bigger thrill in its invention than any other ... the Trent Trotter. It's an odd, unlikely looking thing, I'll readily admit. But in certain circumstances no other piece of tackle could possibly achieve what this float can.

In a nutshell, it's a float for long-trotting extremely shallow swims—and by shallow I mean as little as six inches—at long distances.

I think the best way of helping you understand this little angler's 'must' is by telling you the story of how I came to develop it. And how, finally, a series of accidents occurred which made it more complete than even I had thought possible.

The story began some years ago when I was taking part in the Trent Championship. I had had a bad draw and was placed five pegs below Gunthorpe Weir where the water was extremely shallow as far out as anyone could reasonably throw.

I used a centre-pin reel and although I reckon I can cast as far as any man with one of these, even the mightiest heave was only taking me out to water 12 in. deep at the most.

My only answer in the float department was my regular stand-by, an Avon—which then had a longish crowquill stem and a round cork body about an inch from the tip. I had to use a big one, about nine inches long, to get my bait out. In water only a foot deep, you can imagine how that cramped my style.

By putting a long tail under the float I was just about able to manage and I started to get a few fish. But I suffered badly from the hazard all anglers meet in shallow water like this, back tangles. If I had one, I had dozens—but I remained convinced that this method was the only one on this day which was going to get me any fish.

Then something happened which gave me the first clue on the route that led me finally to the Trent Trotter. I snapped the float stem just below the cork when striking at a fish. That left just a broken stub, the cork and the tip.

Time was running out, so I decided it was too late to change floats. I merely fixed the remains of my Avon back on the line with a valve rubber on the tip and another on the broken stem. I cast in and, to my surprise, began getting much clearer bite indication and more fish. I still suffered the occasional tangle, but it was obviously a great improvement.

At the end of the match I had 7 lb. 12 oz., a catch which won me the Trentman badge for one of the best weights in my zone. I was surprised and delighted and even more determined to master the frustration I'd suffered from this shallow Trent swim. For after all, there were plenty more like it and I might easily draw another the next time.

I realised—it's obvious now!—that my first little accident had permitted me one important advantage. The loss of that long float stem gave me greater leeway at the tail end. This was sufficient for me to use a terminal shot which was far more likely to keep my hook out of the way of the float on the long cast.

Clearly, if I had been able to fish just the Avon's cork body and tip, while still being able to attach it top and bottom, things would have been even better. But that just wasn't possible.

Later, at home, I bore this in mind when I produced my first prototype of the Trotter. The float itself has changed little since that first pattern and is basically an Avon with no stem, except that it has a pear-shaped rather than a round cork body.

But that wasn't all that needed solving. The shotting pattern was something which foxed me for months and finally was only resolved by two more even happier accidents than the first. Even now when I think of how they happened I can't stop a smile ... and a very self-satisfied one at that, I don't mind admitting.

When I first tried out the prototype there was a shot above the float to help me bury the line. But it was fairly close, about 12 inches. All I had beneath the float was one AAA, one inch below it, a BB a little farther down, and a No. 1 shot six inches from the hook.

The rig worked like this, but only up to a point. The big disadvantage was that on the strike the float offered such resistance that any fish I hit were literally hurtled to the surface, causing just the kind of shoal-disturbing splash I was most anxious to avoid in such shallow water.

Time and again, these turbulent strikes sent the shoals away. Nevertheless, I was sure I was catching more fish this way than I would have done with an orthodox float of the Avon type.

Then came the second accident. I was pleasure fishing with the float when I got a tangle which led to the line between rod and float, and the line between the float and the first shot down the line, being held firmly together.

As I was not in a match, and the tangle was a real corker, I carelessly cast in again without making any real attempt to undo it. Within a few minutes I had another bite, but this time the fish wasn't rushed to the surface. Instead I was able to get it out without causing the slightest disturbance to the shoal.

I sat down on my basket for a quiet ponder and after a few minutes realisation dawned. That first shot under the float, because it was gripping the line between rod and float *and* the line between fish and float, was acting like a pendulum. This put me in contact with the fish more quickly and—more important still—reduced the resistance caused by the float on the strike.

I quickly re-set the tackle, pinching both lines cleanly into that first shot. As more fish came to the net I soon found that everytime I struck, the float promptly went straight under and stayed there until I had played the fish well away from the shoal.

But there came a third accident. Although I don't see it as being as important as the first two, it still gave me one of the biggest angling thrills of my life. For it happened on no less an occasion than the National Championship.

It was in the 1961 National in the Trent when, as you must have guessed, I drew one of the shallowest swims in the river. I didn't win but I came near enough in this apparently impossible swim to make me as happy as I've ever been.

When I got to my peg for this match, my heart sank. It was far, far worse than I had expected. I was drawn just above Stoke weir in one of the shallowest reaches of the river. Thirty yards out from the bank it was only a foot deep!

My usual gallery was already waiting for me as I began to tackle up. They seemed to sense it was a tough old swim and one wag called out to me: 'We'll see how good you are today.'

Fortunately, I did have the Trent Trotter and, while I never expected to win a match in the swim, I knew my little float gave me a chance of saving my face at the least.

Little did I realise how much more than that it was going to do for me. The third in a series of accidents with this float was going to happen, in the most important match there is, giving me the last clue to the final shotting pattern you see illustrated here (Fig. 25). But I'm racing ahead.

The wind on this day was distinctly nasty ... downstream and across. It seemed to get stronger as the minutes ticked away to the start of the match. There were titters from behind which I could only take for indications that some of my spectators were really looking forward to seeing me struggle.

I used the Trotter from the start and there were one or

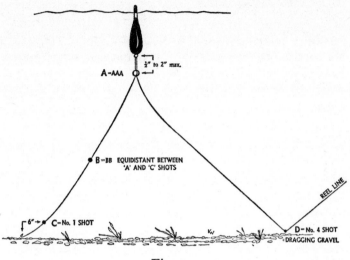

Fig. 25

two sniggers when I produced it for the first time. Maybe it was because it does look a bit like a pilot float for pike that one onlooker was inspired to remark: 'Blimey! He's going pike fishing.'

There were other discomforts at the start of this day. And they got worse. My basket had to rest in six inches of water and every time the lock gates opened I had to move farther out into the river. In one instance I moved out twelve yards.

Once we were 'off' I cheered up for, sure enough, I started getting some fish with the Trotter. I had taken about 4 lb. when it became obvious that the fish in my keepnet were in extreme discomfort because of the shallowness of the water.

I called for the steward who weighed the fish before releasing them. Then, as I had to move forward yet again, the steward dug a hole in the shingle for my keep-net so that there would be water deep enough to hold any fish which followed without damage.

Naturally, all this performing was doing great things for my morale!

But I got stuck in once more and again began catching small fish regularly. At the same time, the wind was slowly, but surely, getting worse making fishing more and more difficult. To give you some idea of how seriously I took it, it's the only match on the Trent I have ever fished with a fixed-spool reel—because of the enormous casts I had to make to get out to the fish.

Because of the worsening wind I moved shot D (see Fig. 25) some four feet away from the float. My only aim was, as before, to sink the line—but quicker.

This turned out to be lucky accident number three with this float. For what happened? I found that I had now got this shot so far from the float it was dragging on the shingle behind the float as I trotted down and—most important of all—was acting like a brake on the tackle.

Just like that it gave me complete control of the tackle in conditions which should have made a mockery of any attempt to fish in them! My only worry was that with this shot so low in the water it would impede the strike. But this did not turn out to be the case. In water this shallow it simply made no difference.

I started to take fish rapidly then but, as so often happens on the Trent, a barge ploughed through and dispersed the shoal. Determined not to be beaten, I immediately began feeding again and twenty minutes later once more started catching roach.

Now I was getting a fish a throw. It seemed unbelievable. At the end I had 17 lb. 4 oz. and that made me fourth individual in the match—a position not one of those people watching, nor even I, would have believed possible at the start.

While my World Championship win and my third in the 1956 Witham National had pleased me greatly, I don't think there was ever a day's fishing in which I felt happier about problems solved than this one. I couldn't stop thinking about that little shot, how I had moved it, and what a tremendous difference it had made to everything. There were so many others in much, much better swims who could have beaten me and I'd beaten them, in what looked the most diabolical piece of water on the entire river.

There were no titters at the end of this match—just the odd gaping mouth here and there. But best of all was the thrill I got the following year when the National Federation of Anglers' annual conference was held in Coventry. Two Nottingham delegates, who had watched me all those months before, came round specially to see me to tell me they would never forget the way in which I had beaten this swim. It was a touching moment.

Having told you the story of how my Trent Trotter came into being I hope I have helped you grasp more easily how it works.

Just to make certain, let's have a little re-cap with the diagram (Fig. 25 again). The first important shot is A. This is the one into which you pinch the line from the reel *and* the line going down to the hook, the shot which gives the tackle that vital pendulum quality which prevents extreme disturbance in the sort of shallow water where the float will be used.

You can see I've made it an alternator and its final position depends on the depth of the swim. The most water you would fish with this rig would be two feet deep, the least six inches. The rule of thumb is that shot A is farthest from the float in the deepest water.

The setting of shots B and C is again determined largely by the prevailing depth. In the diagram the setting is for a swim two feet deep and bear in mind, too, that you fish over depth. In other words, the distance from the float to the hook in these conditions would be 2 ft. 6 in.

In shallower places—say one foot and less—shot B would be moved up to join shot A and, like shot A, would be pinched on to both lines to add to the pendulum effect.

Shot C in two feet of water would be as shown in the diagram. At lower levels, it would be not less than four inches.

You have got to use your own discretion to some extent about the length of tail you fish with this rig. If, for instance, you were fishing with flake for chub in six inches of water you would have a long tail of, say, two feet. But if on the other hand, you were maggot fishing you should keep the tail as short as possible.

Shot D's position can only be judged when you actually begin fishing. The strength of the flow can affect its place for, while you want it to drag the bottom behind the tackle, you want it *only just* dragging and not hard on.

The only yardstick I can offer for this—and it is a real generalisation—is that the distance of shot D above the float is usually exactly twice the depth of the water.

Once you have got the rig set, it is the easiest in the world to fish with. You can cast overhand or underhand. Tangles should be non-existent. Bites will be shown by a crystal clear submerging of the float tip.

Only one thing needs watching after you've started—the speed of the water. If it's very fast you might well find that a heavier shot at point D is needed to give you the right braking effect. But that's the only change you are likely to need.

Now I said when we first began discussing the Trotter that it looks a bit outlandish. But, believe me, it isn't. There is no other tackle which will take fish from shallow running water to come within miles of it ... as I hope the discoveries I've told you about will have proved.

One last word for do-it-yourself float makers. The float is two inches long from tip to base and the body is a pear-shaped cork or piece of balsa half-an-inch at its widest. The tip is cane fitted into the top of the cork. When you've fixed these together all that needs to be added is the float ring at the base.

Chapter *11*

The Trout Trotter

The Trout Trotter is another of my own inventions—
wrongly named, perhaps, for I also use it for chub.

Basically, it's a variation of the small pilot float pike
fishers sometimes use. Its purpose is to permit easy fishing
in fast, shallow water—especially the kind that contains
plenty of obstructions and weed clumps ... swims, in other
words, that most would be inclined to reject as impossible
for float fishing, even with the float we've just discussed,
the Trent Trotter.

When using the Trout Trotter I am, almost without
exception, after trout. A live minnow works a treat with it
on jungly waters like the Windrush, the Evenlode and, until
they banned floats during the close season for coarse fish, on
the Wye and on the Severn.

Exempted from this are the Windrush chub. For I use
this float for them, too, but with flake instead of minnow.

If you don't fish the waters I have mentioned there may
be waters like them in your own area so, first, I think it best
if I tell you more in detail about the kind of conditions this
float is out to beat.

The Windrush is a small but rugged river where the
depth is rarely greater than two feet, much of it completely
broken water rushing forcefully between boulders and
thick weed clumps. In places, it's even weedier than the
Hampshire Avon—a veritable jungle in fact.

The Evenlode, it must be admitted, is more placid having
plenty of sluggish glides. But here, too, there's broken water
and, in places, the most prolific weed growth.

On both these rivers, the only bait I use with this float when fishing for trout is live minnow and, having said that, I'm sure you will now see that the entire rig could best be described as a miniature pike set-up.

For many years I accepted the pilot float—it's like a small *Fishing Gazette* float—as standard for this kind of water. But, as I tried to explain with the Trent Trotter, I found that by attaching the float at the bottom only instead of having it run through the central bore of the float I fished more lightly, more smoothly, and, more important still, disturbed the swim less when striking at a taking fish.

At the same time, you must appreciate that it is a float designed for the shallowest of waters—say between six inches and two feet. Why not, you might ask, merely use the Trent Trotter? The answer is (a) because it is not necessary and (b) because the more complicated shotting of that float is specifically designed for long distance work.

The Trout Trotter is a much simpler job for fishing at much closer quarters.

It is the simplest of rigs (Fig. 26). Look first at shot C. Its placing is not really tied up at all with the buoyancy of the tackle. It is where it is to keep the minnow well down in the water. And its distances from the hook is determined by the depth of the water and the strength of its flow.

Bear in mind, too, that the tackle is always fished over depth, i.e. in two feet of water there'd be a three-foot trace below the float. In really rugged shallow water, shot C would be only six inches from the hook.

To try and make this aspect of the thing clearer: I should never have a trace below the float of less than two feet and if I was reduced to this the water I should be fishing would be only six inches deep. It follows, I hope, that in two feet of water, the cast below the float would be at least four feet.

Shots A and B are lumped together just under the float for two reasons ... to give you weight for casting and to help the float hold up well in rough conditions.

With this rig, you do not keep a tight line from float to rod tip although you do aim to keep in reasonable touch. The

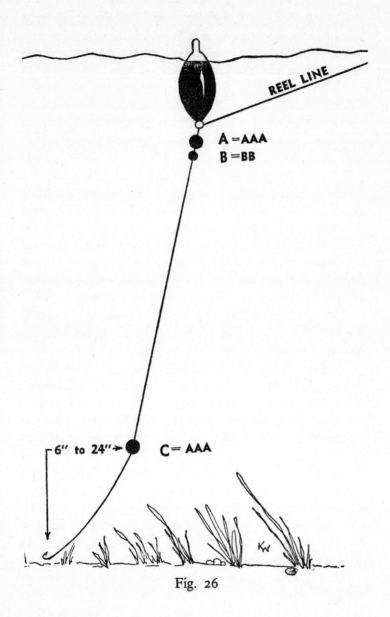

REEL LINE

A = AAA
B = BB

6" to 24"→   C = AAA

Fig. 26

main thing is ensure that the minnow is able to work freely.

It's mostly in winter when I get round to using this float for chub. The shotting arrangement doesn't change and while there's still plenty of foliage about you should find, with a sufficiently large piece of flake coupled with that AAA downstairs, it should pull its own way easily through even the thickest clumps. If you used heavier terminal leads you would have great difficulty guiding the tackle along in this way.

It might be interesting for you to know why I came to reject the ordinary pilot float. First of all, they are generally far too gaudy for working in small waters. The Trout Trotter is dark green with a black tip.

Second, and more important, one found that with the pilot float when working a minnow a fair distance down a small brook some of the line between rod and float would be submerged. The trouble with this being that you never got a really clean strike. With the Trotter this fault is virtually eliminated and the line doesn't wander nearly so much because the float is fastened at the bottom only.

Another point well worth considering is that with a natural minnow a certain amount of control is needed over the bait —but not too much. With some floats the minnow would wander all over the place. But with the Trotter you get just the right kind of control. It roams—but not too far and not too erratically.

Like the Trent Trotter and the zoomer, the Trout Trotter is limited in its uses ... but it's well worth having a couple in your float box for the right occasion.

In fact, it's this kind of comprehensiveness in your float box that I've been trying to aim at all along. Complete the selection I have given you and there's no water anywhere —given various sizes of each float—that you will not be able to beat.

Conclusion

One of the keenest discussions you are ever likely to hear when anglers are talking about floats is the old and still vexed question as to what colour they should be.

It has been said before that the majority of floats in the majority of tackle shops are set out to catch anglers and not fish. This is particularly true of the more gaudy patterns. And as a tackle dealer myself I would go even further. There has never been a time when there were more rubbishy floats on the market than now.

It amazes me that any of them even sell. I stock pretty-looking floats on a small scale in my own shop but I can honestly say that I have never ever recommended them to any of my customers. I value the store they place on my advice too much. On the other hand if they really insist on buying stuff I wouldn't touch then there is nothing anyone can do to stop them.

My own feeling on this question of colour is that the best colour for the body of a float is dark green closely followed by dark brown. These are my personal choices but I would accept any argument favouring any dark colour which could be presumed to offer camouflage.

The finish should most definitely be dull. They may look nicer with a shiny bright varnish on them but not for me. The tip here is to use a dull varnish.

The question of colour for the tip of a float is something else again for this is a factor which depends a great deal on light conditions on the day. If there is a ripple and a shine on the water—especially from the sun—then black for me is the only colour for the tip. If the day is dull and the water comparatively free of ripples then white would be my choice.

I

When conditions are not rough and the sun is behind me then orange or yellow would be my selection.

I am also a great believer in two-colour tips. While my feeling about the extreme end of the tip is unvarying, I also like a second band of colour beneath this one running down below the float's waterline. With a black tip, this band would be white, and with white, orange or yellow tips it would be black.

As I see it, if you have about 1 in. of tip showing and it's of the same colour, a slight lift bite could easily be missed, especially if you are fishing any distance out from the bank. If, on the other hand, you have a two-colour tip that little lift will most often lead to the uncovering of that second colour and then you are in no doubt about what is happening.

Now while my basic tastes are for black or white tips I wouldn't like to be too dogmatic about it because this may be because my eyes may be more sensitive to these colours than anyone else's.

Certainly, in my shop, red easily leads the colours for tip popularity and the presumption must be that customers select it because they can see it better. I would never argue with the man who prefers colours other than my choice for I cannot see with his eyes. The best answer, if you have difficulty with this, is to try as many colours as you can and then stick firmly with the one you have found most suitable regardless of what your friends might say.

All of which brings me to another tip. It is most essential that any self-respecting float angler carries a packet of those interchangeable float tips which are on the market now. They are invaluable for they make a change of colour easy and save the fiddle of tackling down to change the float. They are particularly vital for the match fisherman.

But two things should be borne in mind when using these tips. First of all they are prone to add weight to the float which, particularly when you are fishing light, could mean removing an odd shot to retain balance. Secondly, you can get an air lock in the tip of these covers which tends to make the float sit awkwardly in the water. This is simply because the cover has been put on dry. Wet it first and you will find it slides cleanly on to fit snugly all over the tip.

Make sure every float you own is completely watertight. There is nothing more annoying than to discover after half-an-hour's fishing that your float is waterlogged and sinking all the time as a result. Quill floats are most prone to leak and should be checked regularly for holes, remembering that even the smallest pin prick is enough to spoil them.

Now, in conclusion, I would like to justify my choice of floats in terms of angling logic. Every float dealt with in the preceding chapters was presented for a reason and, now you have read this far, I hope you will have realised why the order in which they were discussed was so deliberate.

My aim was to start at the simplest point moving forward as each new problem called for a new outlook and I think a quick recapitulation is needed here to help you finally get the floats in perspective for if you can understand clearly why I placed them in the order I did, I am sure you will eventually come to select the right float for the right occasion almost by instinct.

The first float we dealt with then was the simple crowquill, a float which, in my opinion, is the basis from which all the other developments have stemmed. Presented with ideal conditions the angler would unhesitatingly pick a crowquill for it is like the essence of float fishing, the ideal.

Unfortunately, this perfect float can only be used when conditions are equally perfect and, as anglers all know, that isn't very often ... which brought us to the next logical stage.

Conditions, we discovered, decide just about everything we do when fishing, especially with floats and particularly when wind is a problem.

Indeed, we found the thing that prevented us using the crowquill was wind—perhaps breeze would be a safer word —which meant that we could no longer hold the bait with the float at the place where we wanted to. We got round this —and keep the logic of it close in your mind—by switching to the reverse crowquill or the dart thus sinking the line and ridding ourselves of wind and surface drag.

But all winds are not breezes and pretty soon we discovered that even these floats, while they sank the line, eventually turned out to be too light to retain casting ability to the chosen spot.

The answer was the onion float, a reverse crowquill with a cork body which meant that distance casting was retained; a facility which could probably be equalled with the dart, too.

Equally significant, in terms of the sequence, the onion was the first float to be used with a body attached.

The reason for the addition of that body was basic to most floats and it's as well to register this thought now ... it gave the float greater buoyancy thus allowing it to hold up better in rougher conditions and permitted the addition of extra shot on the line to make for the same casting distance in a stronger wind.

So far, however, all the floats were answers in still or extremely sluggish water. There followed the problem of running waters.

And it was when we turned to them, the rivers, that we discovered for the first time that it was no longer possible to think in terms of the ideal crowquill. It was simply too delicate for the job in hand.

Our first answer was the Avon family of floats, made these days with cane stems and balsa bodies. Given a selection, these were the perfect floats for fishing streamy waters of all kinds up to a depth of about 8 ft. but there was one thing they would not do—fish well in a downstream wind.

This, then, was our next problem and we solved it by turning to the Duckers, floats which strongly resembled the Avon, but, with their bodies at the lower end of the stem. We found that even with a downstream wind at its worst, the Ducker, in water of similar depths to those specified for the Avon, would do what we wanted it to. It had the added advantage of being capable of the same function in still water, too.

Next in our logical line was the question of what we did

when we encountered water which was too deep to fish with a fixed float, water which, in depth, was beyond the length of our rods. We found the answer to this one in the family of sliding floats.

These, too, we took through the same series of logical problems which faced us earlier with the crowquill through to the Duckers. We found that the sliding float for streamy water was the two-ring sliding porcupine, an extremely useful float for these conditions but one which was next to useless in still waters because of the way in which it seriously inhibited the strike.

The answer here was the sliding antenna fished from the bottom of the float allowing us to bury the line and beat the drag giving us, at the same time, greater casting distance.

I paused there to cope with two small, but important side issues ... streamy conditions in which the two-ring sliding porcupine just would not hold up and close quarters fishing in deep water. Both points were covered by different forms of double ring sliding antennas.

By this stage we had arrived at a point where basically we could deal with most conditions, and the floats which followed were much more specialised—floats for particular occasions which would not be used nearly so often as the patterns which had gone before.

The first of these was the Zoomer, the float which had the same distance casting ability of the sliding antenna in still or sluggish water shallow enough to permit a fixed float making light fishing possible at extreme ranges.

Next came the stick float, the alternative for many to the Avon in streamy waters and ideally for caster fishing. Then came the Trent Trotter which took care of long distance trotting in shallow water, the Trout Trotter doing the same for close quarters fishing especially in shallow streams which were also obstructed.

This then was our logical sequence. All you have to do when considering it is to ask yourself these questions. What is the wind doing? What sort of water have I got—still or running, shallow or deep, fast or slow? How turbulent is the swim? Is it weedy or obstructed? What kind of fish are to be encountered—bottom feeders, surface feeders or mid-water feeders? And whatever the answers are you will find that one of the floats you have just read about will fill the bill.

Finally, I would like to give you a few golden rules for float fishing which have served me in good stead over the years.

And first is the question of materials. In certain chapters I tried to persuade you that some were better for making floats than others.

Let's first consider the crowquill. Any used should be nice and straight and free of leaks. With the exception of my two-ring slider for running water, which is made of porcupine, and the Missile, which uses peacock, I never use any other quill for any of the patterns discussed, though latterly some of them have come to be made of cane instead of with quill stems.

When it comes to float bodies I favour cork for floats with quill stems and balsa for floats with cane stems.

Now in use many floats are abused and I have lost count of the number of times I have walked along riversides only to see perfectly good floats being fished wrongly.

Often it's a case of men using a huge float which is three times larger than the job calls for. The tip here: always use the lightest tackle permitted by the conditions.

Still more will have great chunks of float sticking out of the water—so large no fish could pull it under.

The tip: always make sure that the 'show' on your float is the minimum possible compatible with accurate bite detection.

Shotting is another problem which seems to perplex too many. But it would be no problem at all if only these people would realise that the simple answer is to arm yourself beforehand. In other words when you arrive at the water-side every float in your box should already be accurately shotted so that you can tell at a glance what is needed.

Every float in my creel has got a loop of nylon attached

with the appropriate shots pinched on. The answer is to shot your floats before going fishing in a water butt or bath but when doing so bear in mind the weight which will be below the float when actually fishing of line, hook and bait.

In other words, if you want a $\frac{1}{4}$ in. show on that float when fishing it, its bath tub register should be 5/16ths of an inch.

Another tip is that heavier baits like wheat, cheese and bread paste make a bigger difference to the balance of the tackle than, say, maggot, hempseed or caster so allow the equivalent of a BB when finally shotting the float for use with them.

With regard to shotting patterns, I have been as specific as I could with each float and, with only one exception, the diagrams tell you all you need to know. That exception is when the wind is blowing in your face. When this happens the pattern must be altered for your problem has become one of getting your tackle out while guarding against back tangles round the float.

The answer is to put a heavier shot on down the line in the tell-tale position near the hook. For instance if, before the wind sprang up, you were using a BB in this position you would increase this with a swan at the same time subtracting the appropriate amount to retain the balance from the other shots you have further up the line.

This is particularly simple with all those floats which carry bulk shot—such as the sliders or Duckers. In this case you simply take your big shot—a swan—from the bulk cluster and add the small shot you have removed from the tell-tale to the bulk.

Another tip worth repeating where weighting of floats is concerned—and it applies particularly to those like the onion—is to always carry in your creel a coil of light lead wire. It's so useful and so often can be used to make that last delicate adjustment which shots, sometimes, don't permit.

Always begin your angling day by plumbing the depth. This doesn't need saying to old hands but it's truly remarkable how many anglers don't carry out this vital function. If you know the depth of water and things start happening which affect the way your tackle is behaving, you usually know more clearly what is wrong and what needs changing.

Having taken all these basic precautions gear your mind then to always expect the unexpected. In the normal way it's reasonable to presume that a bite will submerge your float. Alternatively, however, your float may lift. It may quiver. It may move slowly along the surface. A very basic tip then: strike at any unnatural movement of the float. The result may not always be a fish but at least you will always have the satisfaction of knowing that if it was you would have caught it. And all it costs you is the small effort of re-casting.

Which leads me to another important tip: always inspect your bait after retrieving your tackle. For, like me, you are bound to discover that there are times when your bait has been chewed yet there has not been the slightest sign on your float to suggest this. The answer is to move the bottom shot on your line—the tell-tale—nearer the hook. If this doesn't work, and it should in most cases, trying moving this shot in the opposite direction for your tackle might be needing to clear some underwater obstruction you can't see.

Remember, too, that not all the floats I have talked about are designed specifically to go under on the bite. Some will but some are most unlikely to do this. All the sliders, the onion float and all the Duckers invariably lead to lift bites. The tip here: where the body of a float is at the lower end of the stem the tendency to produce lift bites is always greater. Lift bites are also more likely whenever the tell-tale shot is moved nearer the hook.

Casting is particularly important when float fishing. The wrong cast can make the tackle misbehave badly and cause you heartbreaking tangles which, in turn, cost valuable fishing time. The golden rule is to always cast *into* the wind and *never* with it. For instance, if the wind is blowing downstream, cast upstream. The only exception to this: when the wind is blowing from directly behind you then cast straight with it.

As a caster I invariably throw underhand. It takes some mastering, especially when you want to cast constantly and accurately to one chosen spot.

At the same time, I admit that most anglers cast overhand, particularly when fishing big waters. There is nothing wrong with this—my decision to be a permanent underhander is a personal choice—but with certain float tackles overhand casting can be fatal. The tip here: always cast underhand when the body of the float is at the bottom of the stem. A good yardstick: this is almost invariably when you are loose float fishing with the float attached to the line by the bottom ring only.

One general point I would like to make at this final stage is that while I am basically a match fisherman and while the floats I have told you about will do all you could want them to do in a match, they are equally applicable to pleasure fishing. I have the feeling—perhaps wrongly—that the average pleasure angler might feel that these floats might not be for him. He couldn't be more wrong. In fact, I am certain that if the average angler would take the trouble to become conversant with these floats and their use, his catches would treble in the first season which came after and would improve even further in the seasons which followed. And you can consider that a guarantee!

Index